GW00356937

GOVERNANCE AND ACCOUNTABILITY

Power and Responsibility in The Public Service

Editors
Richard Boyle
Tony McNamara

IPA
INSTITUTE OF PUBLIC
ADMINISTRATION

Proceedings of the Institute of Public
Administration National Conference 1997

First published in 1998
by the Institute of Public Administration
57-61 Lansdowne Road
Dublin 4
Ireland

© 1998 with the Institute of Public Administration and with the
authors of their respective chapters.

All rights reserved. No part of this publication may be reproduced
or transmitted in any form or by any means, electronic or
mechanical, including photocopying, recording or any information
storage and retrieval system, without permission in writing from the
publisher.

British Library Cataloguing in Publication Data
A catalogue record for this book is available from the British
Library.

ISBN 1 872002 64 1

Cover designed by Butler Claffey Design, Dun Laoghaire
Typeset by the Institute of Public Administration
Printed by ColourBooks, Dublin

Contents

Foreword

The 1997 National Conference of the Institute of Public Administration, held at Jurys Hotel, Ballsbridge, Dublin, on 7 November 1997, addressed the theme *Governance and Accountability: Power and Responsibility in the Public Service.*

In 1997 a number of Acts were passed which impinge on accountability in the public sector – the Public Service Management Act 1997, the Committee of the Houses of the Oireachtas (Compellability, Privileges and Immunities of Witnesses) Act 1997, the Freedom of Information Act 1997. The Institute was mindful of these developments in choosing the theme for the 1997 conference. Equally, in 1997 there have been developments in practice which suggested governance and accountability as a timely theme – for instance, the planned programme of public service renewal, recent tribunals of enquiry and the creation of new regulatory and monitoring bodies in the public sector.

The presenters at the conference all accepted the existence of new and pressing imperatives to improve the accountability processes of our system of governance. The conference papers, edited and presented in this book, reflect practitioner and academic views. At the practitioner level readers will find a comprehensive guide to recent statutory and administrative initiatives and pointers towards what can be achieved in the immediate future. The contributions from the academics highlight the changed context in which public administration now operates and the challenges presented by change.

Opening Address

An Taoiseach Mr Bertie Ahern TD

It is a particular pleasure to be opening the IPA National Conference in this, its fortieth anniversary year. The contribution which the Institute has made to the development of the public service since 1957 is quite outstanding. Through its education and training programmes, its publishing activities and its research and consultancy work, the IPA has greatly improved the quality of training in the public sector, and has also promoted debate on the key issues affecting the public sector over the years. Because of this, the Institute has played its own unique part in facilitating public service change, and long may it continue to do so.

A shared agenda for change

If we need a perspective on how times have changed since 1957 – the year of the IPA's inception – we need only reflect that the Treaty of Rome was signed in the same year. The European Community has changed almost beyond recognition since then. These changes go beyond expansion of the Community and alterations to the political map. The very nature of government is changing, and nowhere is this more evident than in Ireland. We share this agenda for change with each EU member state, and almost every OECD country.

Over the past ten years in particular, dramatic changes in attitudes, in working roles and in the realm of personal expectations and parity of gender in the workplace have taken place. As Minister for Labour, Minister for Finance, and now Taoiseach, I have been fortunate to have participated in the analysis of change and the development of new strategies to manage that change nationwide, but in a special way in the whole area of the public sector and public service.

I was struck by this shared agenda some weeks ago in Dublin Castle, when I met with a conference of senior officials from central departments and offices of OECD countries. They described the objectives of public management reforms in terms of:

> ...redefining the relationships between government, markets and citizens, in order to achieve a better outcome for the public, at the least possible cost, without compromising core values of equity, probity and effectiveness.

In the context of this relationship between government, markets and citizens, we should be clear what the expectations of government are. Government is expected to:

- contribute the conditions for economic competitiveness and employment;
- promote social inclusion and equity, and deliver efficient high-quality services;
- anticipate trends and conditions;
- strategically position the state's resources accordingly, and optimise the benefits to society;
- legislate effectively and fairly, imposing regulation only when and where absolutely necessary.

In short, government is expected to be part of the solution, not part of the problem. I happen to believe, as citizens, that we are entitled to expect that. I also believe that, as public servants, we can and should deliver nothing less.

Implementing the changes

We are experiencing a time of significant change in the way government does its business. The framework is set out in *Delivering Better Government*, and a key objective is better and more accessible services to citizens. It is interesting to note that the impetus for change comes not only from external sources. I believe that within the civil and public service there is a strong commitment to, and indeed a thirst for, real and lasting change. I base this assertion partly on my own first-hand experience of the public service over the past twenty years, and on the progress we have made with the Strategic Management Initiative (SMI).

The development phase of SMI is now coming to an end. Today, I would like to focus on four elements which are crucial to its implementation:

1   *A clearly-defined set of organisational and divisional objectives, agreed with managers themselves, and supported by a divisional business planning process.*
This will be done through the Public Service Management Act, 1997, which the government commenced from 1 September 1997. The government is about to issue a new set of guidelines for the preparation of strategy statements. Departments will be asked to support them with a meaningful and detailed business planning process, which takes fully into account each division and section, so that there is a shared understanding of objectives and targets, at every level of the organisation.

2   *A workable system of measuring and managing performance, which aligns the strategic objectives of each department or office and division, to individual and team performance.*
This will be achieved through the *performance management* system, which is being developed for roll-out to departments and offices in early 1998. Under this system, individuals will be clear about their role in the organisation, and about the skills and competencies which they need to perform effectively.

3

Performance management will be a continuous process, focusing on personal improvement through training and development.

3   *A financial management system which provides line managers with a common, coherent system of planning and controlling, and taking full responsibility for their resources.*
There will be greater devolution of power and responsibility from the Department of Finance to line departments and offices, through an enhanced administrative budget process, and more delegated authority. Multi-annual budgeting will be a permanent feature of government budgetary policy, to allow us to move from the traditional short-term focus to a more strategic view. The principles of a generic financial model, including whatever changes are necessary to accounting policies, will also be rolled out.

4   *An innovative information technology framework, which will support and empower managers, by providing coherent integration of each of the elements mentioned above.*
The government has asked the new SMI Implementation Group (of secretaries general) to oversee the development of an information technology action plan, which will modernise our information systems in a co-ordinated way. This will include not only the three areas I have mentioned already, but also actions under the Freedom of Information Act, the Quality Customer Service Initiative, and a programme of regulatory reform.

Implications for governance and accountability

I have focused on four specific areas which will impact significantly on public service governance and accountability arrangements 'on the ground'. Other initiatives have also been put in place to strengthen the framework of accountability in Ireland. Many of them will feature in discussion at this conference. They include:

*   The Ethics in Public Office Act, 1995
*   The Public Service Management Act, 1997

- The Freedom of Information Act, 1997

- The Committees of the Houses of the Oireachtas (Compellability, Privileges and Immunities of Witnesses) Act, 1997.

I fully recognise that the Oireachtas has its own important role to play in creating an effective framework of accountability. The arrangements being put in place for the re-constitution of Oireachtas committees in the current Dáil will reflect and enhance the new framework of accountability arising from these legislative changes.

I would also like to mention the Seventeenth Amendment of the Constitution, dealing with cabinet confidentiality, which was approved by the people on 30 October 1997. The amendment will provide for limited exceptions to the absolute confidentiality rule which was the subject of the Supreme Court judgement in 1992. I have said, and I repeat here, that the government will be prepared to look again at the cabinet confidentiality issue arising from the work of the Joint Oireachtas Committee on the Constitution, and the actual operation of the Moriarty and Flood tribunals.

To these I could add a number of measures which I would like to see being advanced in the near future:

- a package of measures on regulatory reform, not only to remove the barriers for important economic sectors such as small and medium enterprises, but to provide clarity and accessibility to ordinary citizens;

- enhancement of the Ombudsman legislation, which will include giving a wider remit to the Ombudsman, to cover all bodies which receive at least 50 per cent of their funding from the Exchequer;

- administrative procedures legislation, to formally assign rights to citizens, regarding the quality and timing of the services which they receive from government departments and offices, and so build on the Quality Customer Service Initiative already in train.

On this last point, I mentioned earlier that quality customer service is a key element of *Delivering Better Government*. Next week, I will launch my department's *Customer Service Action Plan*, and the other government departments and offices will be doing likewise over the coming weeks. These will, for the first time, set out clearly the levels of service to which all government departments and offices are committing themselves. Although simple in concept, I believe this is a very powerful tool of accountability, as it will enable performance to be monitored and assessed in a way which has never before been possible. This will be to the benefit of the customer and the public service alike, and I am confident that the initiative will enable a new relationship to be forged between the customer and the service provider.

From this, I think it quickly becomes clear to us as public servants that the governance and accountability framework in which we operate and transact our everyday business is evolving and quite complex. The real challenge is ensuring that the changes are managed in a coherent and non-threatening way. The key to success here is partnership.

Partnership

I mentioned earlier that the extent of the demand for change within the public service is not to be underestimated. Nor is it, in my experience, confined to particular grades or positions within the system. A commendable – and indeed essential – feature of the modernisation process to date is the partnership ethos which must continue to pervade it. A top-down programme of modernisation has little, if any, chance of effecting lasting change. *Partnership 2000* and the National Partnership Centre are the two 'book-ends' of the partnership approach. In between, there is a range of important measures which we will continue to avail of, to ensure that there is shared ownership of the new framework of governance and accountability.

Conclusion

The three aims which were the starting point for *Delivering Better Government*, and the subsequent modernisation programme can be simply stated:

- excellent service to customer
- maximum contribution to national development
- efficient and effective use of resources.

The changes which are underway, and others which are being considered, are designed to add value to the provision of public services. It is against the yardstick of achieving these three objectives that they must be measured. That is why I said that this conference is both timely and relevant. I wish you every success in your efforts, and my thanks again to the IPA for inviting me to deliver this opening address.

1

Management, Accountability And Public Sector Reform

Professor Andrew Gray

Centre of Public Sector Management Research
University of Durham

There's no question that being a public servant in the new world
is particularly challenging because on the one hand as public
servants we have to learn new disciplines of commercial
relationships and competitive tendering and so on, and at the same
time we must remember the very important traditional public
service values; and that is not an easy combination.

> Ken Jarrold, as Chief Executive, Wessex Regional
> Health Authority; UK, 1993

When Mr Jarrold became Chief Executive of the Wessex Regional
Health Authority in the UK, he inherited a massive management
failure – a huge project designed to integrate computerised information
on all patients and health authority transactions in the whole of his
health region (there were then fourteen in England). It was one of those
schemes designed to put the world to rights, but which failed
spectacularly, partly through misconception of the implementation
required, partly through the impropriety of senior executives and
others involved, especially where there were conflicts of interest
between the interests of the health authority and those of private
commerce, and partly through failing accountability mechanisms.
Although the scheme was introduced in the mid-1980s, it could be

regarded as a warning of some of the problems raised by today's public management.

Taken together these problems suggest that the public sector is providing *the* managerial challenge of our era and is likely to do so for the next decade at least. Why? Because, not only in western industrialised countries but also in the transitional and developing world, the public sector is being diversified as public services are subjected to commercial and related practices to form new mixed economies in their delivery. If for many countries the metaphor of traditional public administration was a railway signalperson faced with one lever operated precisely according to a rule book, today that signalperson is faced with a battery of levers and multiples of combinations to be operated with the guidance of only the most sketchy of manuals.

What then has been going on and what are the implications for accountability and governance? The following paragraphs describe some of the generic changes and raise some of the wider implications. As I was asked to say something of the UK, I will use it as an illustration but refer to other countries as well.

The emerging public management...

The introduction of compulsory competitive tendering in UK local government from 1981 presaged new conceptions of local government as an *enabler* rather than as a *provider* of services[1]. In time this was to affect even the core of professional activity, as social services, planning and finance were subjected to increasingly prescriptive regimes of competitive tendering. This was much more than a genuflection to management fashion at the altar of the private sector; it was part of a long-term and deliberate strategy reflected elsewhere (e.g. in Australia, New Zealand and the USA) to change the way services were being delivered. Borrowing from an influential American treatise of the 1990s, we may describe the process as no less than 'reinventing' public service delivery (Osbourne and Gaebler 1993).

9

What did these reforms seek to change? Historically, the organisation and delivery of government services in the UK and many other western countries were characterised by two main features:

- the development of a career-based system of public service, and
- the organisation and delivery of services by established professionals.

Throughout this traditional system of public administration, politicians (ministers, members of parliament, local councillors) were separated from the delivery of service by the administrative system that neutrally implemented their policies, and in many instances acted as a conduit between politicians and the provider groups who delivered services to the public. With education left to educators, planning to planning officers, policing to police officers, social work to social workers and so on, professional, political and administrative domains were relatively segregated. In this regime *command* was the dominant mode of relationship between politicians and administrators while *communion* was the central element in the professional domain (including relations with service beneficiaries such as patients)[2].

As early as the 1960s, but especially in the mid-1970s, a number of factors undermined this traditional model of public service administration. Long-held criticisms and campaigns for more rational processes of strategic planning, decision making and policy evaluation led to attempts to coordinate and integrate authorities via systems of corporate management (in the UK see Cmnd. 4506, 1970, Bains 1972). By the middle of the decade, however, attention in the UK had shifted sharply in response to a crisis of public expenditure. The British government's view was that policy administrators and professionals alike left financial management to others; as a consequence the use and consumption of resources was neglected. The solution was not some complex planning system but firm financial *control.* As a result, systems of cash limits were followed, after the election of the Conservatives in 1979, by efficiency reviews, financial management initiatives, and resource management regimes. Hence, it can be argued that from the mid-1970s resource management replaced traditional public administration with a consequent shift in the relationships in service delivery.

Although the characteristics of this model varied between and within parts of the public sector, even in the UK, the aim of these reforms was to effect a change in the political control of public services. Politicians sought to extend command into professional domains by injecting more line management into service delivery. In some professional services, such as police and social work, this proved possible within the existing structures; in others, such as health care and higher education, this gave rise to the development of parallel structures of general management.

The emphasis on resource management shared with traditional public administration the offering of a set of value-free arrangements for delivering public services. Resource management, however, was seen as more appropriate to the more complex economic and social environment. It emphasised economy, efficiency and effectiveness, delegated financial management, new decentralised personnel management systems and a strengthening of audit through its certification and value-for-money work. Hence, budgets were delegated, targets set and professionals and other providers designated as 'managers' with responsibilities for delivering activities and services within them. Moreover, the focus included a results-driven personnel management. If traditional public administration was organised as a career service with rewards tied to the position of individuals on complex hierarchical grading structures to which were linked incremental pay spines, the world of accountable management ushered in different possibilities, including a link between reward and performance (as measured by meeting targets) and the local setting of pay and condition regimes.

For the reformers in countries such as New Zealand and the UK, however, the transformation was far from complete. There were thus attempts in both countries to raise further the status and profile of management (and a concept of business-style management at that) as a valued activity in its own right. Although the justification for these further reforms differed (in New Zealand there was a clear theoretical basis in public choice theory, while in the UK the virtue of the private sector was more of an article of faith), the determination undoubtedly provided the political impetus and enthusiasm for privatisation and competition, deregulation and a commitment to customers. Above all, it entailed a subjection of the private world of public service professional monopolies to competition, however that could be contrived. Since the last years of the 1980s, this new public management has intensified the mixed economy in public services. Meeting its challenge has required a new culture of public management.

Thus the last decade has been marked not only by a change of language but also by further complications in the interaction of the political, professional and managerial worlds. In the UK the main instruments for developing new public management have been:

- the structural separation of those providing services from those purchasing them;

- the intensification of competitive tendering: and, more recently,

- the *Citizen's Charter* in all its forms.

Part of the case for decentralising public organisations is the need to force those responsible for delivering services to orientate them toward client needs so that they empower clients and draw them more closely into the policy process. This has been central to initiatives in some UK local authorities (e.g. Tower Hamlets) where both financial and political power has at times been decentralised, and to the *Citizen's Charter*. But this desire to enhance the customer focus (in the broadest sense of the term) is also behind the construction of markets of purchasers and providers within a service (e.g. in community care and education) and the various mechanisms by which many services (including professional) are tested against private sector competition. These markets and variants of market testing bring with them explicit contractual procedures and obligations. So too, though in a less legal but perhaps more visible way, do the citizen's charters.

...and its characteristics

The experience of these quasi-markets and charters illustrates a number of key aspects of today's management of public services in a number of western countries:

- there is a new political environment where policy and management are seen as distinct and separate activities;

- there is a corresponding new internal managerial environment where managers are given freedoms within pre-set frameworks and held accountable against agreed targets;

- new organisational arrangements are designed to facilitate organisational members' identification with the job, a concern with quality and customer needs.

This is a new order of decentralised management within an overall system of central control. For its supporters, it offers scope for the liberation of organisational energy, encouraging local initiative and entrepreneurship and enhancing greater customer or client awareness. It provides a complex overlap and set of interactions between the political, professional, managerial and customer environments and spheres of responsibility. This, in turn, has led to new sources of legitimation in service delivery and new sets of relationships between politicians, providers and authorisers.

If this account is valid, it portrays a world not only considerably removed from that of traditional public administration but also from the simple model offered by market theorists. It is a new world in which public goods and services are provided through more intensively mixed economies than ever before. Its principal characteristics may be elaborated as follows.

Public service organisation
The dominance of traditional bureaucracy has given way to a set of structures of resource allocation and service delivery in which markets, networks and supply chains are as prominent as bureaucracy. Even within the traditional bureaucracy we find flatter hierarchies (the result

of an uncomfortable sounding process known as de-layering) and disaggregated service organisations characterised by designated agencies. At the same time, the dominance of the traditional professionally-based services which emphasise the individual relationship of professional and client has given way to more managerial-based services in which collective organisation and the interests of stakeholders are to the fore.

Public service finance

Many of the traditional public services are now delivered through private sector entities under schemes of privatisation, contracting out or deals involving the provision of capital investment in return for a licence to operate the public service (such as in the UK's Private Finance Initiative). This is breaking down traditional distinctions between private and public sectors. Moreover, less of the service is free of charge at the point of delivery and even where it remains so, more attention is paid to publicising what services cost and who is paying for them.

Public service consumers

The consumer of a public service is seen less as the generic citizen and more the specific client or, increasingly, (paying) customer. If citizens have essentially passive rights they are very much concerned with quality as a processual value expressed through due process and administrative equity. The increasing focus on and empowerment of the paying customer, in contrast, brings very active rights relating directly to the qualities of service at the point of delivery. For service providers to satisfy both sets of rights and conceptions of quality in the same service is a major difficulty[3].

Public service audit, evaluation and regulation

There has been a considerable increase in the amount and manner of audit, evaluation and regulation (well elaborated in Power, 1994). Although some have claimed that accountability has waned as the use of election for public office has declined, there has in many ways been an increase in the liability to present an account, albeit to non-elected accountees. Thus managers find themselves accountable through a greater variety of mechanisms, not only as traditional certification audit has been reinforced by performance audit, but as more use is made of markets and regulatory regimes as evaluators.

Public service practitioners
The challenges for practitioners, collectively and individually – be they managers, professionals or politicians – is the matching of their capacities and abilities to the demands of organisation, finance, consumers and audit as outlined above. In turn there are issues arising for recruitment and selection, including from the private sector, and training and career development. Moreover, these issues have to be managed increasingly through locally determined personnel regimes including contracts, pay and conditions. The effect of all this may be to substitute a public service ethos with a more generic management orientation.

But what of accountability?

In July 1993, William Waldegrave, as Chancellor of the Duchy of Lancaster, vigorously defended the then Conservative government's record of reform against critics who had accused it of reducing accountability and aggravating the democratic deficit. His argument was that, on the contrary, the development of the purchaser-provider split, internal markets for services and citizen's charters was not only increasing the quality of service but itself enhancing the accountability and openness of government. Even if subsequent events have suggested that the British electorate did not share Mr Waldegrave's assessment, he raised an important issue of governance, of application in not only British and Irish systems of government but others too.

So, what has been happening to accountability? The answer requires a recognition that the essence of accountability is an obligation to present an account of and answer for the execution of responsibilities to those who entrusted those responsibilities (Gray 1984; Gray and Jenkins 1993). On this obligation depends the allocation of praise and blame, reward and sanction so often seen as the hallmarks of accountability in action. At the heart of this relationship is stewardship. Stewardship involves two manifest parties: first, the *steward* or accountor, i.e. the party to whom the responsibility is entrusted and who is obliged to present and answer to an account of its execution; and, second, the *principal* or accountee, i.e. the party entrusting the responsibility and to whom the account is presented. Stewardship is thus established when a steward accepts resources and responsibilities entrusted by a principal.

Almost invariably, the steward takes on this trusteeship in return for some reward. In order to gain the reward, the steward must satisfy the principal as to the execution of the stewardship. This adjudication is based on the terms on which the stewardship is established. This brings out the third, latent but equally significant, party in stewardship, i.e. the *code* or codes which govern the establishment, execution and adjudication of the stewardship. By a code we mean an established order or custom which governs behaviour. A code of accountability is thus a system of signals, meanings, and customs which binds the principal and steward in the establishment, execution and adjudication of their relationship. Different codes effect different patterns of accountability. Thus we need to understand their nature and variety if we are to understand public accountability.

Codes of accountability may be characterised in various ways. Internal codes are formulated explicitly to deal with a specific relationship, while external codes have already been established for general categories of relationship (as in professional ethics) and are imported implicitly into specific relationships. Some codes specify standards of outcomes or impacts, others elaborate standards for the process of execution itself (thus the traditional emphasis in public services on due process, regularity and equity of procedure). Codes can be essentially mythical, their acknowledgement being required for displaying symbolically a commitment to certain values (perhaps ministerial responsibility?), or substantive, i.e. designed to govern operational as opposed to reporting behaviour.

One way of characterising such substantive codes is by the rationalities they embody. Thus, following Diesing (1962), codes may promote the adjudication of means in terms of:

- pre-determined ends (technical rationality);
- rules by which social units regulate differences and promote order by, for example, specifying the boundaries of commission and omission, due process and regularity (legal rationality);
- economising, i.e. the economic evaluation of ends and means in circumstances of scarcity (economic rationality);
- the advancement of the integration of the social unit (social rationality);
- the integration of the decision-making system (political rationality).

Although some codes of accountability may appear to embody one of these substantive rationalities to the exclusion of others, in practice the codes comprise combinations, even fusions, of these rationalities. Professional codes, for example, draw on a lateral rather than vertical authority as professional acts are subject to the judgement of peers rather than organisational rules and structures. In this the primary rationalities are technical (means-end effectiveness), legal (the promotion of order), and social (a professional act is justified according to its integration of the profession).

These distinctions are more than mere hair-splitting; they reflect different influences on the practice of public accountability. By recognising them and the model of accountability of which they are a part, we provide ourselves with a framework for examining the effects on accountability of changes brought about by nearly two decades of public management reform.

So what?

The most striking feature of recent public sector reforms is the promotion of accountable management, the underlying principle of which is the delegation to managers of the responsibility for specific resources and the accountability for their use in the pursuit of designated objectives. This implies a framework of objectives and an organisational structure of accountable units to which managers can relate their responsibilities, together with an information system for monitoring and facilitating their audit. Yet some of the reforms themselves, notably the variants of market mechanisms, are claimed to act as surrogates for accountability and thus threaten traditional mechanisms.

The source of this paradox lies in the way the changes have affected codes of accountability by changing the balance of rationalities within them and their interrelationships. There have been changes, for example, in the responsibilities of principal and steward. The latter, e.g. civil service managers, are seen as having become more responsible for their own actions. This applies not only to the use of resources but also more generally to the way civil servants are themselves called to account directly to parliaments, courts and tribunals, as well as within departments. In doing this, the new codes are also more internal to the stewardships in question and thus more explicit. Thus a different managerial code is in use, one which has shifted the balance of responsibilities from ministers to managers and in specific ways.

Further, the reforms have placed more emphasis on technical and economic rationalities at the expense of legal. It could be argued that government organisations have always been charged with economising. However, traditionally much of this has been mythical rather than substantive especially in times (do you remember?) when resources were more freely available. Nowadays, in departments and their agencies, senior managers are expected to plan and appraise resource demands, secure value for money, delegate and control financial authority, and monitor and audit the efficiency as well as the regularity of expenditure.

Finally, these changes are bringing a shift away from *command* and *communion* as the predominant modes of governance towards *contract.* Contract is effected through an inducement-contribution exchange agreed by parties. Legitimacy here derives from the terms of the agreed exchange, i.e. the contract, or at least its interpretations. The strengths of contract lie not only in the pre-determined life of the contract but, more significantly, the motivation to perform up to contract expectation (in order to gain the rewards) and the consequent high probabilities that planning assumptions in inter-party dealings will be acted on. Weaknesses can be traced to the reductionist tendency of contracts, i.e. in the absence of other inducements the parties will limit their actions to those explicitly elaborated in the contract, and the difficulty in the face of changing circumstances in effecting alterations to specification without undue cost.

Of course, public service management relies inherently on combinations of all three modes, and simultaneously in specific situations. Yet, analytically and empirically, particular modes can be associated with identifiable domains of the public service. Thus command is associated with the line management of traditional bureaucracy, communion with service decisions in professionalised sectors and contract with the exchange of goods and services between public service organisations and private entities. Yet the increasing use of market mechanisms and performance regimes (in various guises) have not only enhanced contract as a mode of governance but have come to be regarded as mechanisms of accountability in their own right.

Pity the poor public manager

The overwhelming challenge for public management and the public manager therefore is the accommodation of market mechanisms with the traditions of the public service delivery. Previous research (e.g. Gray and Jenkins 1982, 1991) has suggested that the demands or challenges fall into technical, organisational and political classes:

• The technical requirements of the new public management are those intrinsic to the systems through which services are delivered. Here traditional qualities of analysis must relate to changing mechanisms of markets and networks, and the increasing need to assimilate economic rationalities with traditional legal, political and social reasoning. Of particular significance are technical challenges presented by the contract state, notably legal provisions and risk transfer.

- Organisational requirements are those of structure and process. The developing public management is bringing with it an increasing variety of organisational arrangements calling for not only judgements about the appropriateness of different combinations in particular circumstances, but a facility for handling the human relationships within them. The UK Private Finance Initiative, for example, includes a provision for long-term relationships (perhaps up to twenty or thirty years) between commissioners and private entities providing not just initial capital but operational services. The simplicity of the contract deal disguises a whole series of new relationships both across the deal and within each party to it. Managing the contract state is as much about managing a supply chain as an in-house unit.

- Political requirements are those skills which arise from the macro-political environment in which services are set and to which they must respond (especially in the light of the new government); there will be requirements from the internal political realities of the differentiated interests within the supply chain, and from the challenges to public service ethics. To say that managers have to be able to manage all sets of political demand is not to call for a millennium of Machiavellis but a recognition that management, especially in today's public sector, is still essentially about the management of people and that in turn means politics – in the best sense of the term.

What then is the test of the potential public manager of the twenty-first century? If the challenge is that of managing mixed economies in public services, then Ken Jarrold's twin dicta are appropriate but need a little more. True, the manager must be able to handle the business disciplines which are increasingly underpinning our public services and accommodate these to traditional public sector values. But the premium is on an old virtue: judgement (Vickers, 1965), including distinguishing between strategic choices and contingent responses to strategic imperatives. One of the lessons of Alexander Solzhenitsyn's *One Day in the Life of Ivan Denisovich* was that the prisoner survived the day because he was able, first, to distinguish between an imperative and a choice and, second, develop appropriate modes of action for each. Without judgement, how is the manager to determine these and the appropriate combinations of those traditional management instruments of command, contract and communion? Furthermore, judgement is the quality that protects against universalist prescriptions as a variety of transitional and developing countries seek to emulate the public sector reforms of countries such as the UK and Ireland.

References

Bains Committee (1972). *The New Local Authorities: Management and Structure*, HMSO

Cmnd 4506 (1970). *The Reorganisation of Central Government*, HMSO

Diesing P. (1962). *Reason in Society: five types of decision and their social conditions*, University of Illinois Press: Urbana

Gray A.G. (1984). 'Codes of Accountability and the Presentation of an Account: towards a micro-administrative theory of accountability', *Public Administration Bulletin*, No 46

Gray A.G. and Jenkins W.I. (1982). 'Policy Analysis in British Central Government: the experience of PAR', *Public Administration*, 60/4

Gray A.G. and Jenkins W.I. with A.C. Flynn and B.A. Rutherford (1991). 'The Management of Change in Whitehall: the Experience of the FMI' in *Public Administration*, 69/1

Gray A.G. and Jenkins W.I. (1993). 'Codes of Accountability in the New Public Sector', *Accounting, Auditing and Accountability*, 6/3, 52-67

Gray A.G. and Jenkins W.I. (1995). 'Public Management and the National Health Service' in J.J. Glynn and D.A. Perkins (eds), *Managing Health Care*, pp. 4-32, Saunders

Osborne D. and Gaebler T. (1993). *Reinventing Government*, Plume Books

Power M. (1994). *The Audit Explosion*, Demos

Vickers G. (1965). *The Art of Judgement*, Penguin

Notes

1. For a fuller account see Gray and Jenkins 1995

2. *Command* is based on the rule of law emanating from a sovereign body and delivered through a scalar chain of superior and subordinate authority. Legitimacy for public service decisions and behaviours under such governance lies in their being within the bounds prescribed through due process by the institutions charged with the provision. This is a traditional characteristic of bureaucracy in public service. Its strengths lie in the efficiency and effectiveness of control and accountability; its weakness in rigidity and conservatism in the face of changing environments. *Communion* is based on an appeal to common values and creeds. Here legitimacy for actions lies in their consistency with the understandings, protocols and guiding values of a shared frame of reference. Its strength as governance lies in the guidance afforded by its shared values through different environments; its weakness is its insularity from those environments and a consequent failure to adapt its normative order.

3. One of my research students, a senior local government manager, reports that in town planning, for example, the same service has to provide for the paying customer, who makes an application for a house extension and expects a direct, speedy and personal service, and the applicant's neighbours, who expect due process, participation and deliberation!

2

Accountability To The Citizen

Kevin Murphy
Ombudsman and Information Commissioner Designate

Introduction

When I started to prepare this paper, I asked myself the question 'What do citizens want of their government and public administration?' Of course, they want a myriad of things, depending on who they are and what particular hat they may be wearing at the time. Citizens are taxpayers, mortgage holders, social welfare recipients, members of the travelling community, employees, politicians, business people, drug addicts, prison inmates; they are young, old, middle-aged, healthy, sick, disabled; they are men, women, poor, rich, informed, uninformed ... one could go on indefinitely.

Just as in economics, where overall demand curves are derived from the preference curves of individuals, so, it seems to me, it is possible to state generally what citizens expect of public administration. I believe that citizens want a public administration in which they have confidence because they know that, by and large, it is honest, it is fair, it is responsive to them and inclusive of them, it is efficient and gives value for money, it is effective in that it produces results or outcomes which increase the welfare of the community as a whole, economically, socially and environmentally.

This confidence, which is the lubrication which ensures a properly working democracy, can be secured only if public administration is open, transparent and accountable and if there are effective mechanisms in place to ensure this. In the Irish context, the most important mechanisms have been, and will continue to be, the Houses of the Oireachtas and the courts. Added to these is the mechanism of public scrutiny in which the media play a vital role. Shortcomings in the effectiveness of parliamentary control of government and public administration have been evident for some time, while the expense and slowness of litigation has inhibited the effectiveness of access to the courts. A number of steps have been, and are being, taken to improve matters, such as the new committee system in the Dáil, the Committees of the Houses of the Oireachtas (Compellability, Privileges and Immunities of Witnesses) Act, 1997 and the restructuring of the administration of the courts. While these are welcome, there is much which remains to be done. In my view, there is a need for more research and enquiry into how the two great institutions of state, the Oireachtas and the courts, can be made more effective in ensuring the greater accountability to citizens of government and public administration. As to the media, questions have been raised concerning the suitability and the ethics of their being used (or sometimes abused) as a mechanism of accountability. This is not the occasion on which to address that complex issue, nor do I claim the competence to do so.

Ad hoc tribunals of enquiry have, of course, been used in specific cases as a means of filling these gaps in accountability. In addition, in very many countries new independent institutions have been created operating, in a manner of speaking, in the twilight zone between parliament and the courts. In Ireland, the Comptroller and Auditor General has been there since the beginning of the state to help the Dáil in its efforts to ensure that public resources are used correctly, properly, efficiently and, in more recent times, effectively. This office has been joined since 1984 by the Ombudsman, since 1989 by the Data Protection Commissioner, since 1995 by the Public Offices Commission and from April of next year by the Information Commissioner under the Freedom of Information Act, 1997. All these offices enjoy considerable powers both to investigate and to secure remedies. And, of course, we have also had three ad hoc commissions on referendum information.

In this paper, I will deal mainly with my role as Ombudsman in trying to ensure accountability to the citizen. First of all, I will say a few words about the role of the Public Offices Commission in ensuring ethical accountability and about the importance of access to information in facilitating public scrutiny of government decision making.

Standards in public life and The Public Offices Commission

The Ethics in Public Office Act, 1995 established the Public Offices Commission on 1 November 1995. The five member commission comprises the Ombudsman, the Ceann Comhairle, the Comptroller and Auditor General, the Clerk of the Dáil and the Clerk of the Seanad. My office provides the secretariat to the commission. The Act provides for the disclosure of interests by holders of certain public offices, such as Ministers and members of the Oireachtas, and other persons holding designated positions or directorships in the public service. It also deals with gifts to ministers and personal appointments by them. The commission also has a role under the Electoral Act, 1997 in relation to disclosure of political donations. The provisions of these pieces of legislation are aimed at ensuring integrity in public life by requiring greater transparency in the area of interests, gifts and donations and, inter alia, the relationship between government and business.

The Public Offices Commission has considerable powers of investigation where alleged breaches of the Ethics Act occur; these powers are comparable to those of a tribunal. Actions which took place before the commencement date of both the Ethics and the Electoral Acts are, of course, outside the commission's jurisdiction. To date, no complaints of breaches of either Act have been received by the commission.

A further mechanism which other countries have adopted to ensure transparency is, of course, 'whistleblowing' – the disclosure by public servants of unethical activities combined with protection against retaliation for the 'whistleblower'. There are many difficult issues involved in such a mechanism including ethical questions and the possible divisive effects on the public body concerned. I would also pose the question, in the context of a buoyant Irish economy and greater movement from the senior public service to the private sector, as to whether we need to develop a formal code of practice to regulate such movement.

Access to information and the Information Commissioner

In less than six months time, April 1998, the Freedom of Information Act, 1997 will come into effect and it will confer new responsibilities upon me in my additional role as Information Commissioner. The Act aims to replace the culture of secrecy in the public service with one of openness. The purpose of the Act is to enable the public to obtain access, to the greatest extent possible consistent with the public interest and the right to privacy, to information in the possession of public bodies. The Act confers the following new legal rights on members of the public:

- the right to seek access to information held by public bodies (including information in relation to themselves);
- the right to have personal information held by a public body amended where it is incorrect or misleading (and this right applies regardless of whether the material is held in a manual or a computer record);
- the right to seek reasons for decisions affecting themselves.

My job as Information Commissioner will be to ensure that the public's right to know is upheld and not hindered in any way. My functions may be summarised as follows:

- to review (on application) existing decisions in relation to freedom of Information (FOI) requests and to make binding new decisions;
- to keep the operation of the Act under review with a view to ensuring maximum compliance;

- to foster an attitude of openness among public bodies by encouraging the voluntary publication by them of information on their activities which goes beyond what they are obliged to publish under the Act;

- to prepare and publish commentaries on the practical operation of the Act;

- to publish an annual report which will be laid before the Houses of the Oireachtas.

Public interest test

Most of the exemptions defined in the Freedom of Information Act are subject to an overriding public interest test. There is no definition of the public interest in the Act and decisions taken by public bodies or by the Information Commissioner on this issue will be a matter of judgement based on the facts of each individual case. In many cases, the respective arguments for and against disclosure will be finely balanced. It will be necessary for public bodies to demonstrate to me as Information Commissioner how the public interest would be either harmed or not served by the release of the information. Without prejudice to any individual decision, I consider that such decisions should be taken against the background of the purposes of the Act. While the Act contains no specific purpose clause – unlike the position in New Zealand and Australia – there would be general agreement that the Act is designed:

- to extend, as far as possible, the right of the community to have access to information in the possession of public bodies;

- to make government more accountable by making it more open to public scrutiny;

- to improve the quality of political democracy by giving the opportunity to all citizens to participate fully in the political process including the formulation of policy;

- to enable groups and individuals to be kept informed of the functioning of the decision-making process as it affects them and to know the criteria which will be applied by government agencies in making those decisions; and

- to enable individuals to have access, except in very limited and exceptional circumstances, to information about them held by public bodies, so that they may know the basis on which decisions, which can fundamentally affect their lives, are made and may have the opportunity of correcting information which is untrue or misleading.

The ad hoc commissions on referendum information

Before I leave the subject of information, I would like to offer a few personal comments on the activities of the three ad hoc commissions on referendum information. These commissions, comprising the Ombudsman, the Clerk of the Dáil and the Clerk of the Seanad, were asked by successive governments to supervise the preparation by two senior counsel of statements for and against the amendments to the Constitution in relation to divorce, bail and cabinet confidentiality. Let me say straight away that I strongly support the principle of citizens being given the maximum amount of information to enable them to make informed voting decisions. In the case of the divorce referendum, we produced a booklet which set out the case for and the case against the amendment and we sent it out to every household in the state. In the other two referenda, there was no option because of very tight time constraints but to set out the respective arguments by way of advertisements in the national and provincial newspapers. This had the merit, or demerit, depending on your viewpoint, of requiring brevity but even brevity came at a quite considerable cost – close to £400,000 in each case – and more than double the cost of the procedure used in the divorce referendum. Furthermore, the supply of information was limited to readers of newspapers. I cannot claim to be satisfied that our efforts were successful and there is clearly room for improvement but I think the general approach is right.

Referendum on the Amsterdam Treaty

I am raising this question now because I believe serious consideration needs to be given immediately to how the referendum on the Amsterdam Treaty is to be handled. This is not a single issue referendum which lends itself to a repeat of the simple procedure of brief statements prepared by senior counsel. There are a number of very important but also very complex issues affecting our future which will need to be explained and clarified for the public, apart altogether from the merits of the issues themselves. One could envisage a series of booklets setting out in a clear and objective way the background to each issue and its rationale, and then going on to give the arguments for and against the proposed amendment. I cannot see how these booklets can be successfully produced without the involvement of the civil service. Yet because of the Supreme Court's judgement in the McKenna case there is a clear reluctance on the part of the government and the civil service to give out any information – even factual information – relating to a referendum. It seems to me that, if the final drafts of the booklets are vetted and approved by a new independent commission with access to a broad spectrum of expertise, the objective of ensuring a balanced exposé of both sides of the argument for a change in the Constitution would be met. I have every reason to feel that the civil service would be capable of participating in this process in a constructive and neutral way. The neutrality of the civil service is recognised, for example, in briefings for political parties in the run-up to general elections, and ways could be found for their participation in an objective fashion in such a process. There is, of course, the danger of information overload for citizens if the supply is not spread over a period of months. It is essential, therefore, to reach a conclusion at an early date as to how the dissemination of information is to be handled in the run-up to this important referendum. With adequate notice, it should also be possible to exploit the potential of the other mass communications technologies, including radio and television, in order to ensure that the public is well informed.

Administrative accountability and the ombudsman

I define administrative accountability as the process of ensuring that public service activities and, in particular, the exercise of decision-making powers, whether discretionary or otherwise, are carried out not only in a proper legal manner but in a manner consistent with fairness and good administrative practice.

In short, I am there to decide whether or not public bodies are guilty of maladministration. Just as financial auditors examine the activities of the public service against certain financial principles and criteria, I examine their activities against the background of what are commonly referred to as the principles of good administration. I outlined these principles in my annual report for 1994 and I also published a charter of citizens' rights in dealing with the public service. I elaborated on these principles of good administration in my 1995 annual report and illustrated their relevance to the individual complaints which came before me. In my 1996 annual report, I published a *Guide to Standards of Best Practice for Public Servants* setting out in plain language what needs to be done if citizens are to be dealt with properly, fairly and impartially by the public service. These 'accountability parameters' are derived from the categories of maladministration given at Section 4(2)(b) of the Ombudsman Act, 1980, from the practical experiences of thousands of complainants and from Ombudsman colleagues throughout the world.

Fair treatment

My role as Ombudsman is not simply a question of ensuring a better quality service to customers or clients. While obviously I have a shared interest with public bodies in ensuring better service, my interest goes deeper than that. If any section of the community feels that the system treats it unfairly, and that there is no accessible avenue of redress, then that confidence in public administration so essential to democracy will be missing. Greater efficiency and cost-effectiveness are, of course, key elements which the public service must pursue but it must never be forgotten that, unlike his or her counterpart in the private sector, the user of public services seldom has a choice of an alternative competitive supplier. Fair treatment is vital and must not be lost sight of when efficiency measures are being introduced. In addition, the pressures on individual public servants arising from greater commercialisation and greater personal accountability for performance must not lead to any diminution of public service values.

In trying to ensure that public servants are held accountable for their administrative decisions, the Ombudsman acts at a number of levels. At one level accountability for individual decisions is achieved by the examination and investigation of individual complaints and the provision of redress where justified. Since the Office was established, 46,000 complaints have been handled and in approximately 40 per cent of cases some form of redress has been achieved. Examination of individual complaints often leads to the identification of systemic defects in procedures, approach or even attitudes and at this level valuable feedback can be given to the bodies within my remit. Procedures and systems can then be improved in order to ensure that particular complaints do not recur. There is, however, a further level to which I attach particular importance – identifying and seeking remedies for deficiencies or injustices which have become endemic in the public service culture, and which contribute to that 'democratic deficit' which everyone admits exists and which alienates the citizen from the institutions of state.

Areas of concern

Let me deal with four areas of concern to me, each of which has a bearing on the question of accountability:

- bad communications and record keeping;
- misuse of delegated legislation;
- adversarial attitudes; and
- gaps in the protection of human rights.

Bad communications and record keeping

The public service still seems to have difficulty in providing adequate information and giving clear and simple reasons why a particular decision was taken. Deficient communications are the cause of many complaints which come to my office. The charter of citizen's rights which I published in my 1994 annual report identified the following rights for citizens in their dealings with public bodies:

- the right to be heard;
- the right to receive sufficient information;
- the right to assistance and representation;
- the right to be given reasons;
- the right to be told what remedies are available to them.

I am hopeful that the Freedom of Information Act, 1997 and especially Section 18 (which gives citizens the right to look for and get reasons) will dramatically improve this area.

One example of poor record keeping is shown in a complaint against Wicklow County Council which I dealt with last year. The case resulted in changes in the information management practices of that body. The complainant claimed that a document present in a planning file was not on the file when it had been inspected earlier; as a result, a submission to An Bord Pleanála did not deal with the points raised in the 'missing' document. In accordance with my suggestion, the council agreed to number and index planning files with effect from 1 January 1997 so that callers to the planning office could be confident that they had seen all documents relating to the file. I also wrote to the Department of the Environment and Local Government suggesting that it should issue a general circular to all local authorities on this aspect of planning file maintenance. The Freedom of Information Act at Section 15(5) provides for the enactment of regulations governing the management and maintenance of records. As the above example demonstrates, such regulations will have an important role to play in eliminating the maladministration involved in missing or incomplete records.

Misuse of delegated legislation

The second concern relates to the area of delegated or secondary legislation of which there is a vast and growing amount. Here I have found that restrictions or qualifications, not specifically provided for in the primary legislation, are often incorporated into statutory regulations which as we all know receive very little scrutiny, since most of them simply need to be laid before the Houses of the Oireachtas to have effect. I detect an attitude which sees delegated legislation as a means of fine tuning in areas which might prove controversial if included in the primary legislation. I will give you two examples:

Example 1: Claims and payments regulations
The Social Welfare (Consolidation) Act, 1993, provides for the making of regulations which would disqualify persons from getting a benefit if they fail to claim in time, but goes on to allow the time limit to be extended. The clear intention was to get people to apply in time in the interests of proper administration and good financial management, but to allow late claimants who had good reasons for not applying in time to be dealt with reasonably. Yet the regulations provided that, irrespective of the reason for the delay in claiming, arrears payments would be limited to a maximum of six months. In some cases where, for example, people did not apply because of physical or mental ill-health, they suffered considerable financial penalties which could not be justified on any notion of equity. Yet from the Department of Social, Community and Family Affairs point of view the law was the law and they saw themselves as having no discretion. Taking to heart George Bernard Shaw's statement that 'The reasonable man adapts himself to the world, the unreasonable one persists in trying to adapt the world to himself. Therefore, all progress depends on the unreasonable man', I decided to investigate. Without going into the details of my investigation into this matter – which incidentally is the first investigation report to be published

in full by my office – I can say that up to a hundred claimants have now received arrears and, in addition, the minister has indicated that he will be amending the regulation to ensure that penalties for late claims have regard to individual circumstances. In my report I quoted the Council of Europe view on the principle of equality before the law:

> The principle of equality before the law does not mean that the administrative authorities should not carefully and fairly consider each individual case by reference to the applicable laws and rules. The law should not be drawn up so as to prevent the administrative authorities from treating every case in a manner appropriate to its circumstances.

Example 2: The nursing home subventions regulations

In 1990 the Oireachtas enacted the Health (Nursing Homes) Act, 1990 which, inter alia, provided for the payment of subventions to 'dependent persons' in private nursing homes. The Act, at Section 7, provided that the Minister for Health might, by regulation, prescribe the amounts to be paid by way of subvention and that the amounts '... may be specified by reference to specified degrees of dependency, specified means or circumstances of dependent persons or such other matters as the minister considers appropriate'. On the face of it, there is nothing unusual about all of this. But when the Act commenced in 1993, following the making of regulations in relation to subventions and other issues, something quite unusual emerged.

The minister's regulation defined the term 'circumstances' as the '... capacity of a son and/or daughter, aged twenty-one years and over residing in the jurisdiction, ... to contribute towards the cost of nursing home care of his or her parent'. On the basis of the interpretation of the regulation relied upon by most of the health boards, the practical consequence has been that subvention decisions take account of the capacity of a son or daughter to contribute to a parent's nursing home costs. The subvention otherwise payable is reduced by the amount by which a son or daughter is considered by the health board to be in a position to contribute. And this line is generally taken irrespective of whether the son or daughter wishes to contribute, is actually contributing, or is contributing at a rate less than the health board's figure. In effect, the regulation is being generally operated as if the adult children had an *obligation* to contribute to the parent's nursing home costs.

As far as I am aware, there is no statutory obligation on children to support their elderly parents. The Health (Nursing Homes) Act does not create any such obligation and, from my reading of it, there is nothing in that Act to suggest such an obligation. Nor is there anything in that Act to suggest that the term 'circumstances' should be defined in the way it has been defined by the regulation.

It may, or may not, be desirable that children should support their elderly parents. I believe that in Germany, for example, there is some such obligation. Whether or not we should have such a provision is a matter for the Oireachtas. What concerns me here is that the minister, and his department, appear to have created a *de facto* obligation to support as between children and their elderly parents without any discussion on this issue in the Houses of the Oireachtas, thereby avoiding effective accountability.

This is an issue which I am continuing to examine.

I expressed my general concern about delegated legislation in a submission to the All-Party Committee on the Constitution established in July 1996. I referred to the Constitution Review Group's recommendation that consideration be given to an amendment to Article 15.2.1 of the Constitution so that the Oireachtas should have power to authorise, by law, the delegation of power to either the government or a minister to legislate using the mechanism of a statutory instrument. I consider that such legislative decisions would be essentially administrative in nature and, therefore, should clearly be seen to be within my remit as Ombudsman.

Adversarial attitudes

The third area of concern to me is an attitude I find prevalent among some public bodies, particularly in the local government and health areas, to complaints where payment of compensation is likely to be a factor. There is almost a knee-jerk reaction to the effect that this matter is more appropriate to the courts than to the Ombudsman. This attitude is, I suspect, influenced by their legal advisers who are steeped in the adversarial system. But there is an arrogance about the view which I find disquieting. It treats as adversaries the very citizens whom public bodies are elected or appointed to serve. It also ignores the provisions of the Ombudsman Act which permit me to recommend '... that measures or specified measures be taken to remedy, mitigate or alter the adverse affect of the (public body's) action ...'. There are no financial or other limits on what I may recommend and no restriction on my dealing with complaints which could involve very large sums of damages. This adversarial view also assumes a level playing field, which clearly does not exist, between the individual complainant and a large organisation with its own legal and other expertise. As Hogan and Morgan state in their seminal work on administrative law:

> ... the structure of our law on the judicial review of administrative action is – perhaps inevitably – so designed as to exclude from its scope many cases of injustice arising from maladministration. Moreover, the High Court ... is an expensive and inaccessible place. The result is that relatively few instances of maladministration surface as court cases. [*Administrative Law in Ireland*, Hogan and Morgan, 1991, p.279.]

Indeed, recent experience should suggest to public bodies that an adversarial approach may be very costly in the longer term. It is for these reasons that I have included in my *Guide to Standards of Best Practice* the admonition that public bodies should not adopt an adversarial approach as a matter of course where there may be a fear of litigation. One such case, which I describe in more detail in my 1996 annual report, illustrates my point. The complaint came from a couple whose house had been flooded; they said that they had spoken to Galway County Council on a number of occasions about the risk of flooding from surface water running from the nearby road and that they had asked that steps be taken to rectify the situation. No preventative action had been taken, however, and the ground floor of their house was flooded. The complainants contended that the council had failed in its obligation to maintain a blocked roadside culvert and drainage pipe near their property, and that this failure resulted in the flooding of their home causing damage estimated at £3,000. In response to the complainants' claim for compensation, the council said that as there was no negligence on its part, it would not pay compensation. The council maintained throughout that the claim should have been dealt with through the courts. Following an examination of the complaint by my office, the council reviewed its decision at my request and concluded that it had a *bona fide* defence to the claim on the following grounds:

- there had been exceptionally heavy rain at the time and the council had successfully defended all resultant claims through the courts (this latter claim subsequently turned out to be incorrect);

- the flooding, or most of it, had been due to internal drainage;

- the complainant may have made an unauthorised connection to the roadside culvert.

I was not satisfied with the council's response and decided to investigate; my recommendation was that the council pay the complainants half the cost of restoring the house and the council accepted this.

Gaps in the protection of human rights

The final area of concern to me is the area of human rights. At European level there are now regular meetings and contacts between Ombudsmen and the institutions of the Council of Europe concerned with human rights. It now appears likely that a Council of Europe Commissioner for Human Rights will be appointed. There is also growing co-operation at world level between Ombudsmen and the United Nations High Commissioner for Human Rights (Mrs Mary Robinson) and her staff. The Ombudsman institution is increasingly recognised as an effective instrument for the protection and promotion of human rights especially in Latin America where the Spanish model of Defensor del Pueblo is used but also in the new democracies of Eastern Europe.

In Ireland, the institution of Ombudsman is not generally perceived as being involved with the protection of human rights, possibly because of the strong provisions in the Constitution governing personal rights and the active role played by the courts in their enforcement and development. I have tried, since taking up office, to stress that citizens have rights vis-à-vis governmental and public bodies and that these bodies often, consciously or unconsciously, deny people their human rights in social, economic, health and property matters. People particularly at risk would include members of the travelling community and people with disabilities, as well as refugees, asylum seekers and immigrants who, while not yet citizens, still have human rights. Property owners too can be affected and my office has received complaints from householders who have been unable to sell or develop their property due to the long term road plans of local authorities. As the law stands, there is nothing I can do to assist these complainants; there is clearly a need, however, for a mechanism whereby compensation for the loss in market value caused by the action of the local authority could be considered.

In my contacts with the Council of Europe, I have been taken with the growing importance for all my colleagues of the rights of refugees, asylum seekers and immigrants as well as of persons deprived of their liberty whether it be in custody, in prison or in mental institutions. Among the immigrant/refugee population, my Ombudsman colleagues tell me that the single biggest source of complaint is the question of delay in dealing with their applications. Other complaints relate to the manner of interviewing applicants, the provision of interpreters and natural justice considerations. Of course, all of these complaints can be construed as maladministration, but under Section 5(1)(e) of the Ombudsman Act, 1980, I am precluded from examining complaints concerning the administration of the law relating to aliens or naturalisation.

In their consideration of whether we should have a Human Rights Commission in Ireland, a majority of the Constitutional Review Group came down in favour of a statutory commission without any adjudicative role. Complaints of human rights violations should continue, in their view, to be determined by the courts. I am not convinced that this is necessarily the right course and I feel that much more debate and analysis of developments elsewhere in Europe would be desirable before conclusions are reached at political level.

Conclusion

In conclusion I must emphasise that external review bodies such as the Ombudsman or the Public Offices Commission are not a substitute for proper values and mechanisms 'in house'. There is a continuing need for standards to be set from the top down and for proper internal appeal and audit systems. Finally, and in anticipation of the question: 'What do citizens want of their Ombudsman?', could I answer that they expect him – or her – to be:

- clearly independent in doing the job;
- accessible to the public with as few formalities as possible and at no cost to them;
- fair in dealing with complainants and also with the public bodies which are investigated; and
- effective in securing appropriate redress when justified.

I am delighted that my annual report has been the subject of debate in both Houses of the Oireachtas by the elected representatives of the people and that there was a clear consensus that the Office of the Ombudsman continues to be a worthwhile addition to the mechanisms of accountability.

What Can We Do In Order To Establish A Culture Of Performance Management?

Jacques Toulemonde

*Centre for European Evaluation Expertise
and ENTE - Lyon*

Since 1997, Irish spending departments must carry out systematic performance reviews. The Minister for Finance is putting in place agreements with public managers in the form of three-year review frameworks. This process is aimed at improving the performance of government services and activities. It relies heavily upon two assumptions: (1) it is possible to measure performance in a credible way within public organisations, and (2) public managers are prepared to facilitate this measure and to learn from what performance measurement shows. Anyone who has worked in the civil service, in any country, will realise that these assumptions should not be immediately taken for truth.

What makes them credible is that Ireland is far from being the only place in the world where they are accepted. New Zealand and Australia have paved the way. Government performance review is an exploding activity in America, under the pressure of President Clinton's administration. Jacques Santer has put performance measurement at the top of the European Commission's agenda through the *SEM 2000* initiative (Sound and Efficient Management). At present, anybody who wants to speak of public administration in an international arena must learn and use the language of performance management.

However, the history of management fashions shows that several years are typically required for putting a new language into practice and for establishing a new organisational culture. In order to understand how to establish a culture of performance management, it is worth looking backwards at the experience of democratic countries where deliberate policies have attempted to promote a new administrative culture. This is the aim of this paper.

In the language of public performance management, the term 'evaluation' plays a central role. Monitoring and evaluation are the basic tools for measuring performance. This paper will take for granted that evaluation is capable of measuring public performance (assumption 1). The reader whose confidence in that statement needs to be strengthened may find many arguments in the international literature (Boyle, 1996, Mayne et al., 1997, OECD, 1996).

In this paper, I will develop and assess the second assumption: public managers are prepared to facilitate performance measurement through evaluation and to learn from evaluation findings.

As with any other innovative practice, evaluation grows through an interactive process requiring a skilled professional community on the supply side and a group of committed consumers on the demand side. It is not realistic to assume that evaluation fulfils an existing demand in the public sector. On the contrary, demand must be created and progressively developed at the same pace as supply, if not faster. The following pages address the question of how evaluation demand has been promoted in various countries. The main focus is on the instruments that evaluation promoters can manipulate in order to create and to nurture the demand. Hereafter, these instruments are presented with the help of the metaphor of carrots, sticks and sermons (Bemelmans-Videc et al., 1997).

An individualistic model of the decision to evaluate

I start with a model that explains evaluation demand from the individualistic standpoint of a decision-maker who is assumed to behave in accordance with the balance of positive and negative consequences of his/her choice. The subject of the reasoning is any person who has to decide upon the evaluation of a programme, to ask an evaluative question, to open a door for data collection or to accept the conclusion of a report. The model applies to someone who is practically capable of supporting or blocking an evaluation at any one of its stages. The reasoning is analysed with the help of a 'decision tree' with a trunk and six branches (see Diagram 1).

In Diagram 1 the decision process is illustrated, with the first decision to be made at the base of the trunk whether to evaluate or not. The trunk has two main branches: 'yes' and 'no'. The 'yes' branch always has a direct cost, whatever the conclusion of the report. An example of direct costs is the time and money spent in the evaluation process. By contrast, the 'no' branch normally involves no direct cost or any other indirect consequence. The 'yes' branch is always a problematic compound of assumed costs and benefits, while the 'no' branch is appealing because of its simple neutrality.

Diagram 1: The evaluation decision tree

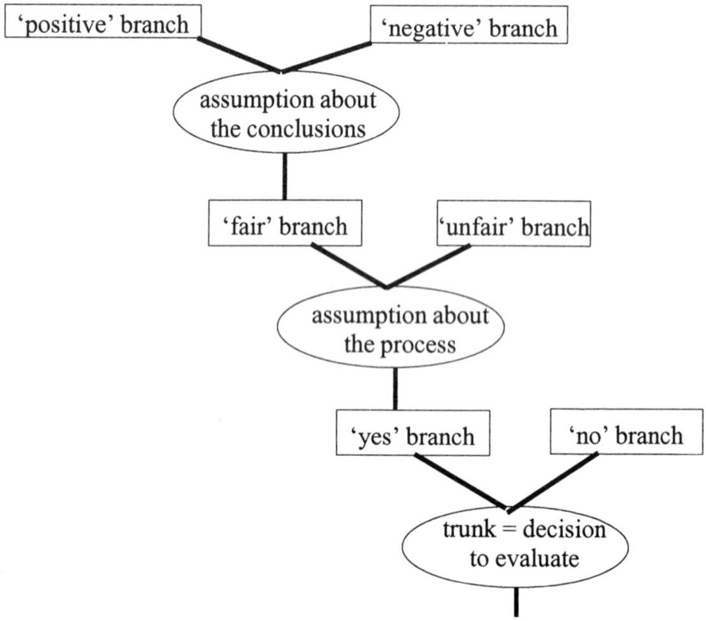

In many cases, evaluation demand has been developed by manipulating the attractiveness of both branches. The principle is to put carrots on the 'yes' branch and sticks on the 'no' branch. An example is the system of the French *Contrats de Plan Etat-Région* (CPER) (see Box 1). In order to encourage regional authorities to evaluate, the promoters of the system reduced the direct cost of evaluation in several ways. First, the national government decided to retain 0.06 per cent from its financial commitments within the CPER and to earmark this money for evaluation. It was proposed that the regions do the same from their side. The 0.06 per cent levy acted as a powerful incentive, removing the cost barrier to evaluation demand. The system then created another incentive and removed another barrier by proposing that state-region evaluation committees keep control over the publication of evaluation reports. This allowed regional authorities to protect themselves against the risk of losing control over strategic information. Only after this facility was given did the most reluctant regions agree to play the evaluation game.

Box 1 - The French *Contrats de Plan Etat-Région* (CPER)

The French State-Region joint plans (CPERs) are agreed every five years through a negotiation process involving the French government and each of the twenty-six regional governments. A CPER consists of a plan that harmonises major public programmes funded by both levels of government in almost all policy fields. Although several rounds of CPERs have already taken place, the first evaluation system was set up in 1993. In each region, national and regional authorities establish an evaluation work plan which is implemented in partnership. A national scientific committee is in charge of an ex-ante assessment of the quality of evaluations. In the framework of this system, evaluation practice amounts to about fifty reports per year.

(This experience has not yet been reported in English in the scientific literature)

In Australia, the decision was made to put some sticks on the 'no' branch. The Australian Public Service Evaluation System was set up by the federal executive in 1988. This regime applies to all federal portfolios. As in Ireland, it is strongly promoted by the Department of Finance. Evaluation practice amounts to ten to twenty reports a year. Portfolios (departments) are required to issue evaluation plans. This creates a cost of not doing evaluation, namely a need to spend time and energy in explaining why a programme should not be submitted to evaluation (Mackay, 1993, Sedgwick S.T. 1992).

Assumption about the evaluation process ('fair' or 'unfair')

If the 'yes' branch is chosen, the next two branches relate to the fairness of the evaluation process. A 'fair' process is likely to strengthen the network of people who have stakes in the programme, making the decision to evaluate more attractive. By contrast, doubts as to the fairness of evaluation make the whole game unpredictable. The conclusion of an 'unfair' evaluation depends on the powers and tactical skills of the various players, something which is extremely difficult to foresee. In this case, the only reasonable behaviour is to resist, either actively or passively, and to opt for the 'no' branch of the decision tree, no matter how many incentives or constraints apply to its other branches. Fairness is a particularly sensitive issue since evaluators have to make explicit value judgements without being equipped with ready-to-use criteria and benchmarks. Fairness can seldom be taken for granted, especially in the first years of the development of evaluation when deontological/ethical rules, quality standards and professionalisation are not fully established. This explains why confidence is a basic ingredient of evaluation demand.

From this standpoint, an interesting arrangement is that of the French *Conseil Scientifique de l'Evaluation* (CSE) (see Box 2).

Box 2 - The French CSE – *Conseil Scientifique de l'Evaluation*

In 1990 the executive branch at national level established an evaluation system which provides for several large evaluations per year, each of them involving several ministers. Evaluation projects are initiated by ministers on a voluntary basis in almost all policy fields. The ministers who initiate these projects must submit their draft terms of reference to an ex-ante quality assessment by a Scientific Council of Evaluation (CSE). Once agreed, the evaluation projects benefit from the support of a National Fund for Evaluation Development which amounts to FRF 4 million per year (ECU 0.6 million). The CSE also carries out ex-post quality control at the final report stage. In the framework of this system, evaluation practice amounts to about five reports per year.

More details in: Nioche J.P. (1992) and Duran P., Monnier E. and Smith A. (1995).

The ministers who initiate evaluation projects must submit their draft terms of reference to an ex-ante quality assessment. Up to now, the CSE has assessed twenty-eight evaluation projects. It has at times rejected individual evaluative questions or even rejected complete evaluation projects which partly overlooked the views of some stakeholders or were not of an evaluative nature. The CSE also carries out ex-post quality control at the final report stage. During its six years in operation, it has established rules of the game that ensure a fair evaluation process i.e. involves key stakeholders in an evaluation group, presents intermediary reports to the evaluation group, separates fact-finding and analysis by consultants from judgement making by the evaluation group, and so forth. The CSE has eleven members, half of them being top civil servants and the other half well-respected academics. Its role as guarantor partly explains why numerous evaluation demands have appeared within a system that relies solely upon volunteers.

The example of the Audit Commission for England and Wales (ACEW) illustrates another way of securing fairness which is more informal and pragmatic. The commission was created by the British government in order to ensure that local authorities made proper arrangements for achieving economy, efficiency and effectiveness in the management of their resources. Since the context was one of reducing the autonomy of local authorities, the ACEW's activities risked being seen as unfair. Nevertheless, it managed to create confidence in evaluation by developing close cooperation with those under evaluation and by including among its members people with past and present connections with local authorities. An important part of its success derives from its choice of evaluation topics relevant to the needs of local authorities. Evaluation teams often comprise top managers or other senior people nominated from local authorities.

These two examples show how fairness can be secured either by a compulsory system of quality assessment (stick), or by a highly participative approach to evaluation (carrot).

Prediction about the evaluation conclusions (positive or negative)

If the evaluation process can be considered as 'fair' and if the 'yes' branch is chosen, the highest branches of the decision tree relate to the evaluation report itself: will it shed a good or a bad light on the programme? Decision makers always make their own intuitive assessment of the programme under evaluation, which shapes their opinion on whether a fair report will judge the programme favourably or not. They will strongly anticipate a favourable report if they personally support the programme, while opponents of the programme will expect criticism.

The ultimate consequences of the evaluation for an individual stakeholder depend on whether or not the report is in line with his/her expectations. A favourable report leads to 'positive' consequences for a programme supporter, as a critical report does for a programme opponent. Since almost all people involved with evaluation demand have stakes in the programme, some of them will inevitably fear negative consequences while others will expect positive ones.

Box 3 - The Dutch Reconsideration of Public Expenditures (RPE)

The Reconsideration of Public Expenditures was set up in 1981 when the Dutch government set up a procedure of systematic reviews aimed at cutting back public expenditure in all policy fields. The RPE is organised in annual rounds. Each round includes from ten to fifteen evaluation studies which are agreed through full cabinet decisions. Each evaluation is the responsibility of a specially appointed inter-departmental working group. The latter receive central steering and secretarial assistance from the Ministry of Finance. They are not required to speak with a single voice and the final report may include opposing points of view. Evaluations are issued in connection with the budgetary process and must include an alternative programme proposing a 20 per cent saving in the budget. During the first decade of the RPE, about one third of the evaluation results were directly used to reduce budgets. No clear pattern has been found to explain this successful utilisation. It did not result from an especially high quality of the evaluation reports, nor from an especially low level of resistance by bureaucrats. The Dutch system uses many constraints, such as centrally-decided evaluation plans and systematic proposals of budget cuts. Nevertheless, these constraints are applied in a flexible way and stakeholders are involved in the evaluation process with some degree of freedom. This smart use of sticks has created a sustained evaluation activity, of which a reasonable proportion has proved to be useful.

More details in: Bemelmans-Videc M.L. (1989) and Nisper van tot Pannerden F. (1994).

Only 'pure' neutral administrators, evenly agreeing to kill bad programmes and continue good ones, would always feel that evaluation has 'positive' consequences. The problem with ultimate consequences is that they can hardly be manipulated. Critical reports and/or negative consequences inherently belong to the evaluation game and there is no point in introducing a bias in favour of complacent evaluation. Evaluation promoters must accept a kind of 'law of symmetry' which states that some programmes are good and others not, that evaluators measure good performances in some programmes and poor performances in others, and that evaluation satisfies some stakeholders and not others. When a country tends to link evaluation and budgetary allocation, the law of symmetry also applies so that good programmes are likely to have their budget increased and bad programmes are threatened by budget cuts (e.g. the Netherlands – see Box 3). Structured feed-back mechanisms make the 'positive' branch more attractive and the 'negative' one more frightening. If such mechanisms apply to a large number of evaluations, they are likely to generate a greater number of both supporters and opponents of evaluation, in a symmetric way. That is why linking budgeting and evaluation is a very difficult task (see Gray et al., 1993).

In the search for new instruments to manipulate evaluation demand, one can link budgeting and evaluation in an asymmetrical way. This idea emerged in Colombia when all departments were submitted to systematic budget cuts. The national planning agency suggested that a few programmes could escape the budget cuts provided they demonstrate good achievements through evaluation. I suggested a similar idea in the framework of a recent evaluation in Belgium (European Commission, 1995). A 1,500 million ECU programme was under evaluation and the funding authorities planned to allocate a complementary budget amounting to 5 per cent of the programme. The evaluation was designed to influence the allocation of this additional budget. In the Colombian case, as in the Belgian one, the evaluation itself does not generate a risk of budgetary cuts. The process is turned into a positive sum game with the aim of creating a co-operative attitude among stakeholders towards evaluation.

Decentralisation is another strategy that can be applied to ensure that the ultimate consequences of evaluation are always seen as 'positive', and to sustain evaluation demand. It enables decision makers to master all the consequences of an evaluation report, whether their programme is eventually judged as good or bad. Decentralised evaluation looks like self-evaluation or like what Fetterman (1994) proposes under the label of 'empowerment evaluation'. It is a powerful instrument of evaluation development that should not be forgotten. Some interesting features of the strategy exist in the evaluation system of the Job Training Partnership Act in the USA (see Box 4). This system included a rule of compulsory evaluation but the practical arrangements for evaluation were left entirely to the initiative of the states which had to set up the organisational arrangements. No guidelines were issued at federal level. An attempt to undertake a large national evaluation project met with a considerable amount of political resistance. By contrast, decentralised projects appeared to grow successfully, at least in quantity. In less than ten years, nearly 190 evaluation studies were carried out. State and local evaluators came together in a network which initiated training workshops. The network promoters published several guidelines, as well as 'Evaluation Forum', a special journal whose title neatly illustrates the decentralised way of developing evaluation.

Box 4 - The Job Training Partnership Act in the USA (JTPA)

The Job Training Partnership Act (JTPA) was adopted by the Congress of the USA in 1982. The JTPA was implemented by the states, in association with local authorities and private sector organisations. Federal funding was divided up between the states on the basis of needs indicators. As regards the local programmes, the role of agents at the federal level was limited to defining targets and performance standards, and to participating in monitoring and evaluation. In the framework of this system, evaluation practice amounted to about twenty reports per year.

More details in: Upjohn Institute for Employment Research (1990).

In search of the proper mix of constraints and incentives

It is now possible to summarise how incentives and constraints can apply to the various branches of the decision tree proposed in Diagram 1. The following recipes have been tried and proven:

- obligation to establish an evaluation work plan: a stick that makes the 'no' branch more difficult;

- provision of money earmarked for evaluation: a carrot that makes the 'yes' branch more attractive;

- right to keep evaluation information under control: a carrot that makes the 'yes' branch more attractive;

- systematic quality assessment: a stick that makes the 'unfair' branch more unlikely;

- systematic consultation and involvement of stakeholders: a carrot that makes the 'fair' branch more likely;

- decentralisation: a carrot that helps decision makers to assume 'positive' consequences.

This list of recipes shows that constraints and incentives can be mixed and applied to all factors of evaluation demand. The art of combining the various instruments is illustrated by two French examples below.

The French governmental evaluation system (see Box 2) relies heavily upon demand from ministers. This demand has been successfully manipulated by means of two instruments: a carrot on the 'yes' branch (National Fund for the Development of Evaluation) and a guarantee of 'fair' evaluation (Scientific Council of Evaluation). Nevertheless, the system has not proved to be very convincing and after six years in operation its future is far from certain. Its weaknesses appear when one looks at the nature of the evaluations which have been undertaken to date. The first evaluation dealt with the effects of computers in the civil service, a topic hardly likely to disrupt the political agenda, and was followed by many other subjects of equally minor importance. The financial carrot and the guarantee of fairness have successfully created a demand for evaluation. However, these instruments have not been powerful enough to overcome the reluctance of the bureaucracy to address politically sensitive issues, or the collective avoidance of conflicts which prevail in some political circles. The lesson from this example is that a certain degree of constraint needs to be applied; at least a few sticks should be included in the mix of instruments.

The evaluation system of the Rhône-Alpes region has achieved a better balance of sticks and carrots. It was born in 1990 when the regional council (legislative branch) obliged the regional executive to set up an evaluation system. This potentially conflicting origin is not, however, visible in the features of a system which has turned out to be highly participative. The executive branch produces annual evaluation work plans, each of which covers about four major regional programmes. Programme managers are closely involved in the framing of the evaluation questions. Once decided, the evaluation process is open to all major political leaders, including opponents in the regional council, and to representatives of the relevant lobbies. Up to fifty stakeholders gather in an evaluation group which holds four or five meetings during the evaluation process. These meetings are, moreover, surprisingly well attended. A scientific committee is responsible for validating the methodological quality and ensuring the fairness of regional evaluations. Sticks are not absent from the system which, all in all, runs fairly smoothly. Recently, the regional council requested the executive to publicly respond to the conclusions of an evaluation. The evaluation system had proved capable of creating a collective interest and a spirit of confidence in the evaluation work. It was easily renewed after the first three years in operation.

Conclusions

Evaluation demand develops faster when incentives and constraints are mixed and applied to all branches of the decision tree. But, one must go further than this. If some clever promoters were capable of manipulating all relevant carrots and sticks, would this suffice to overcome all political and bureaucratic resistance to evaluation? The answer is clearly no.

There will always be instances where people involved with evaluation demand predict dramatically 'negative' consequences of evaluation, like the death of their programme, the destruction of their legitimacy or even the loss of their jobs. If an evaluation function is anchored in another part of the institutional setting rather than the programme, such a risky evaluation can be effectively supported. Nevertheless, if such drastic threats hang from the top branches of the decision tree, all the other branches will simply be forgotten by those who fear evaluation, no matter what incentives and constraints they offer. From their point of view, incentives will simply be neglected and constraints will systematically be resisted or turned around. This explains why even the best mix of carrots and sticks will never eradicate the pockets of resistance to evaluation.

Evaluation demand and culture-building (sermon)

Let us imagine why a decision-maker might opt for evaluation when this dramatically contradicts his/her self-interest, and let us call this reason 'goodwill'. Is there any instrument which can be manipulated in order to develop this goodwill? Such an instrument does indeed exist: it is the building of an evaluation culture. Once this culture is well established, evaluation is deeply rooted in the administrative values, is seen as an undisputed duty and becomes one of the fundamentals of the governing system. The culture provides the collective pressure that makes decision makers overcome their reluctance, even when evaluation deeply contradicts their self-interest.

Establishing an evaluation culture requires more than an intense and sustained communication effort. Its success depends less on the content of the message or the quality of communication techniques than on how well-respected the messengers are and how many colleagues have already been convinced. In a certain sense, the process of developing an evaluation culture resembles that of preaching faith: the 'sermon' seems to be the relevant instrument. In the context of public administration, sermons take the form of conferences, workshops, training courses, newsletters and journals. They make extensive use of demonstration projects, success stories, visits to good practitioners, prizes and awards. Those who listen to the sermon should be convinced that they belong to a community of people who trust that evaluation is part of sound public management.

Civil servants should become proud of their job when they evaluate. The evaluation culture of a decisionmaker relies very much upon the social pressure exerted by his/her colleagues. In a certain sense, one should apply the same type of instrument in building an evaluation culture as in launching a new management fashion.

At the end of this review of international experiences, the lesson which emerges is that all instruments should be applied together: incentives, constraints and culture building. In order to create an evaluation demand, one must use carrots, sticks and sermons altogether. This conclusion is well illustrated by the case of Australia which boosted evaluation practice most effectively through a clever mix of all three. Major Australian programmes are required to be evaluated every three to five years in the framework of rolling annual 'Portfolio Evaluation Plans' (sticks). The Department of Finance supplies consultancy services and staff support to evaluation demanders (carrots). Many civil servants belong to evaluation networks and since 1991 more than 2,500 officials have attended one-day evaluation workshops. An evaluation register is published and now covers 500 reports (sermons). An observer of Australian practice considers that evaluation contributes to job satisfaction in the civil service by increasing the belief that programmes can be improved (Mackay, 1993). A series of surveys carried out between 1991 and 1994 shows that out of the new policy proposals, up to 77 per cent (1994-95) were influenced by evaluations. While clever evaluation promoters use carrots and sticks at all branches of the evaluation decision tree, they also acknowledge that nothing except sermons can overcome human resistance in the most difficult cases.

Such an all-embracing and general conclusion might not be of much help for those who start building an evaluation system and have to choose the first stone. Very often at this early stage many instruments are simply not available. Can we start building an evaluation system if constraint is unthinkable? Can we keep developing evaluation demand if there is a shortage of carrots? When looking at the various national experiences, it seems that some success can be obtained when evaluation promoters are limited in their capacity to manipulate the various instruments. Their weaknesses simply result in a slower development of evaluation demand. This happened in the Swiss example (see Box 5). The Swiss constitutional setting involves so many checks and balances that evaluation promoters were unable to manipulate constraints and incentives. Their major instrument was the dissemination of evaluation knowledge and they also tried to build an evaluation culture. Their efforts led to obvious – albeit very slow – progress in evaluation practice though they did not fully achieve the setting up of a Swiss evaluation system.

Box 5 - The Swiss *Groupe de travail d'Evaluation Législative* (AGEVAL)

In 1987, the Swiss Federal Department of Justice and Police set up a Working Group on Law Evaluation (AGEVAL). The group included members of both the executive and legislative branches at federal level, representatives of the cantons, and high-level academics. From 1987 to 1991 the AGEVAL held twelve meetings. The same Federal Department of Justice and Police also initiated a research programme on the impact of federal measures (PNR 27) which was launched in 1987 by the Federal Council with a CHF 5 million (ECU 3 million) budget over seven years. This research programme applied to all policy fields, not only those of Justice and Police. After almost ten years, no evaluation system formally exists in Switzerland. Swiss evaluation practice can be estimated at around ten to twenty reports per year.

More details in : Bussmann W. (1995).

Contrasting the Australian and Swiss examples, one can conclude that it is possible to develop a large and sustainable evaluation capacity on the demand side in less than ten years, provided that all instruments are available for manipulation. Progress will be slower if some instruments are missing.

References

Bemelmans-Videc M.L. (1989). 'Dutch experience in the utilisation of evaluation research: the procedure of reconsideration', *Knowledge in Society*, 2, 4, 31-48

Bemelmans-Videc M.L., Rist R.C. and Vedung E. (1997). *Carrots, Sticks and Sermons: Policy instruments and their Evaluation*, New Brunswick, NJ: Transaction Publishers

Boyle Richard (1996). *Measuring civil service performance: designing and using performance indicators in the Irish civil service*, Dublin: Institute of Public Administration

Bussmann W. (1995). 'Evaluation and Grassroots Politics: The Case of Switzerland', *Knowledge and Policy*, 8, 3, 85-98

Derlien H.U. (1990). 'Genesis and Structure of Evaluation Efforts in Comparative Perspective' in Rist R.C. (ed), *Programme evaluation and the management of government: patterns and prospects across eight nations*, New Brunswick, NJ: Transaction Publishers

Duran P., Monnier E. and Smith A. (1995). 'Evaluation à la française: towards a new relationship between social science and public action', *Evaluation: the International Journal of Theory, Research and Practice*, 1,1,45-63

European Commission (1995). 'Applying the Multi-criteria Method to the Evaluation of Structural Programmes', *MEANS Handbook* 4, Brussels: European Commission – DG XVI

Fetterman D.M. (1994). 'Empowerment evaluation', *Evaluation Practice*, 15, 1-15

Gray A., Jenkins B. and Segsworth B. (1993). *Budgeting, Auditing and Evaluation: Functions and Integration in Seven Governments*, New Brunswick, NJ: Transaction Publishers

Mayne, J., Zapico-Goni, E. (eds) (1997). *Monitoring Performance in the Public Sector*, New Brunswick :Transaction Publishers

Nioche J.P. (1992). 'Institutionalizing Evaluations in France: Skating on Thin Ice' in J. Mayne et al. (ed) *Advancing Public Policy Evaluation: Learning from International Experiences*, Amsterdam: Elsevier Science Publishers, 23-36

Nisper (van) tot Pannerden F. (1994). *Het dossier Heroverweging*, Delft

OECD (1994). *Performance Management in Public Administration*, PUMA Studies no. 3

Toulemonde J. (1996). 'Europe and the Member States: Cooperating and Competing on Evaluation Grounds', in Rieper O. and Toulemonde J. (ed), *Politics and Practice of Intergovernmental Evaluation*, New Brunswick, NJ: Transaction Publishers

Upjohn Institute for Employment Research (1990). *Evaluating Social Programmes at State and Local Level*, Kalamazoo

Evaluation And Measurement Of Government Performance – A Local Government View

William Soffe
County Manager, Fingal County Council

Four core principles are presented in *Better Local Government – A Programme for Change (1996)*:

* enhancing local democracy

* serving the customer better

* developing efficiency

* providing proper resources.

Two of these are particularly relevant to the issues which we are discussing to-day. These are – *serving the customer better* and *developing efficiency*. In the programme they were elaborated upon as follows:

* serving the customer better through
    – a focus on the needs of the customer;
    – timely delivery of services of high quality, measured against *performance indicators*;
    – personnel training and development in customer care;
    – rigorous but streamlined operation of the various regulatory controls, and

- more openness and transparency in decision making in local authorities;
- developing efficiency through
  - a modern and progressive financial accounting system with an increased emphasis on costing services;
  - development of *performance* and *financial indicators* and *value-for-money* audit;
  - development of strategic management;
  - development of partnership between central and local authorities, and between local authorities and other local organisations; and
  - effective use of information technology on a planned basis.

In charting the future direction of local government, the programme seeks to move progressively towards a system which among other things provides efficient services.

At this stage, local authorities generally have, in their strategic management plans, accepted this as the future approach to the delivery of local government services. In our case in Fingal, our plan is in the common format, setting out:

- our mission
- our values
- our objectives
- our strategies

for the next five years.

Part of our mission is to provide high quality services for all the people of Fingal. Two of the values which we will uphold are:

Quality of service
Our over-riding priority is to provide an *efficient, effective, reliable* and *courteous service* for all our customers, guided by high *ethical standards.*

Value for money

We will aim to provide the most *economic service* and obtain *value for money* at all times.

We, in common with all other local authorities, are clear about the direction in which we must go. The next phase, in which we are now engaged, is the preparation of detailed action plans to implement our strategies. This work includes the formulation of *performance indicators* for our services.

Arrangements to monitor and review the plan on a regular basis will be established to ensure that action plans will be implemented in accordance with the strategy.

It goes without saying that we in the public service operate in an entirely different environment from private sector organisations. In our case, in local government, there are several important national factors which affect performance and its management and evaluation. For example:

• government financial policy

• Department of the Environment and Local Government directives

• national pay agreements in relation to pay and conditions

• statutory financial demands over which the local authorities have little or no control.

On the local front, performance can be significantly affected for better or worse by a number of other factors:

• the political complexion of the council

• the financial capacity of the authority

• the make-up of the population of the administrative area

• the geography of the area.

None of these factors can be used by the local authorities as an excuse for not embracing performance evaluation and measurement enthusiastically. They simply illustrate the need for an approach specifically tailored to the nature of our business; and we must accept that we are in a service business with owners/customers to whom we have to explain increasingly what we are doing and why.

Could I now turn to the detail of what a system of performance evaluation and measurement for local authorities might look like. At the outset, can I say I am firmly of the view that whatever system we adopt it must be an evolving one; it is just not going to be possible to have, from day one, a fully-developed sophisticated system.

It needs to have the three elements which Jacques Toulemonde talks about – a careful mixture of *incentives* (carrots), *constraints* (sticks) and *culture building* (sermons).

A well-signposted feature of the new local government funding arrangements is the proposed linking of allocations to efficiency and value for money. So, those local authorities which perform to a high standard will be rewarded and those who do not will lose out. The third element – *culture building* – is particularly vital. All of us in local government, elected members, management and staff, have to accept the concept of performance evaluation and measurement because government and our customers want it.

In a statement in July 1995, the government said that it believed that a renewed system of local government can provide a more effective focus for the effective delivery of a wide range of public services for the better development and well-being of local communities, and for promoting more local development and enterprise. By its performance local government must justify that belief.

It seems to me that any local authority system should have at least the following three categories of performance measures:

- services management
- financial management
- customer/citizen measures.

Measures or targets under these headings should be constructed in such a way that valid comparisons between the performances of the various local authorities can be made.

In relation to *services measurement* we should concentrate in the beginning on the main infrastructural and planning/development services, with a small number of measures or targets and build on those. Possible areas suitable for performance measurement might be:

• non national roads maintenance/improvement costs

• water production and distribution costs

• refuse collection and disposal costs

• timescale for dealing with planning applications

• sewerage collection and treatment costs

• housing maintenance unit cost.

It will be essential to set down clear standards for levels of service against which performance can be measured, as well as taking into account the differing capacities and resources of authorities.

In relation to *financial management* performance measurement might relate to:

• operating within annual expenditure and income budgets;

• meeting revenue collection targets;

• management of capital budgets;

• expansion of sources of funding.

With regard to *citizen/customer measures*, initiatives under this heading must be included in any system of performance measurement and evaluation for local authorities and indeed for all branches of the public sector. Possible measures might be:

• response rate for water supply defects/failures

• response rate for housing repairs

- response rate for the issuing of motor tax/driving licences
- timescales for replying to correspondence
- timescales for answering telephones/phone queries
- response times for emergency calls.

It is feasible under these three categories to construct a system of performance measurement and evaluation which will assess the efficiency and effectiveness of an individual local authority and facilitate comparison of local authorities with each other.

It will be more difficult to measure and evaluate us (both individually and collectively) under policy headings, mainly because the local authority is not often sufficiently in control of performance. Areas I have in mind are:

- implementation of the recommendations in *Better Local Government*
- making a new development plan
- making a waste management plan
- implementation of the government's sustainability strategy.

In spite of the difficulties involved, some weight should be given to performance in these areas in evaluating the overall performance of local authorities individually and collectively.

All of the possible areas for measurement I have mentioned so far can be seen as applicable to local authorities generally. The question has to be addressed as to whether measures or targets should also be set, within a scheme, for the implementation of special local projects. Examples in the case of Fingal County Council might be:

- the construction of the Balbriggan by-pass
- the upgrading and extension of Leixlip waterworks
- the construction/extension of Malahide, Swords and Balbriggan/Skerries sewerage schemes.

It is quite feasible to evaluate and measure projects such as these but, since all local authorities would not have similar or comparable projects, they cannot effectively be used widely for comparative purposes.

The evaluation and measurement of an organisation's performance must include the evaluation and measurement of the performance of its staff. Efficiency, effectiveness and value for money in a local authority must be delivered by the manager and staff of the authority in partnership with the elected members.

The changes planned in *Better Local Government* require radical changes in human resources structures and management in local authorities. Up to now, our HR management has been grounded, as the 'Purple Book' says, on standardisation effected through central government prescription and control. The new approach signalled in the programme is based on local authorities having the freedom to manage their human resources, within budget, to deliver more effective services to the public. This will involve:

- fundamental changes in the local authority staff structures
- more team working
- the introduction of performance related pay, firstly for managers, and perhaps then down through the grading structures
- the extension of the short-term contract arrangements.

The achievement of these changes present difficult IR challenges. However, I believe that local authority staff recognise and accept the need for fundamental changes in structures and work practices. They will welcome having their performance compared with that of their counterparts in the private sector but they will, of course, seek to have their pay and benefits compared also.

Who will be the evaluators?
Performance evaluation and measurement will lead to considerable bitterness and strife unless it is fair and seen to be fair. No matter how one sets measures and targets, evaluation cannot be simply a

mathematical exercise. There will be a sizeable element of subjective judgement. So the selection of evaluation teams must be given great care and attention. A possible structure might have a steering group comprising

- an independent chairperson
- a senior official from the Department of the Environment and Local Government
- a local authority lord mayor/cathaoirleach
- a local authority manager
- a small number of representatives of our customers
- a representative of staff organisations.

It would also be advisable to have a team of external evaluators to carry out the evaluations

- in accordance with a clear set of guidelines prepared by the Department of the Environment and Local Government in consultation with the stakeholders involved
- under the direction of the steering group.

Conclusion

Local authorities, in my opinion, perform well and over the years have provided a high standard of services with limited resources. That is not to say that there is not room for improvement – and in that we are no different from any other organisation.

We have no reason to fear performance evaluation and measurement, so let us get on with implementing a performance evaluation and measurement system which has *measures* which are

- both quantitative and qualitative,
- cover the areas of services, finance and customer focus, and where possible
- cover also the policy and special project areas.

This must be done with a system which has acceptable independent evaluation structures and is linked to performance measures in government departments which affect the freedom of the local authorities to perform.

5

Independent Regulation: Governance and Accountability

Etain Doyle
Director of Telecommunications Regulation

Introduction

As first Director of Telecommunications Regulation, I am very pleased to have the opportunity to discuss the key issues involved in developing the Regulator's role, and establishing its position in relation to the industry and government agencies.

Public management structures in Ireland are currently undergoing major changes as part of the general renewal programme for delivering better government. The objective is to put in place suitable organisations and management processes to ensure that the public service is capable of meeting the challenges of the present and of the new millennium. The establishment of the Office of the Director of Telecommunications Regulation (ODTR) is a clear example of this.

It is an example on 'fast forward'. It has now the opportunities and responsibilities of independent exercise of functions within a legislative framework. Its structure has been developed to deal with the particular regulatory challenge it faces. The industry it serves is also on 'fast forward' as Ireland seeks to catch up with telecommunications developments in other countries.

A sea change is starting in the public service, a sea change which will match the development of the Celtic Tiger in its profound implications for Ireland and how we do business. The ODTR is in the vanguard of this change. This paper is devoted to reviewing the role of the ODTR and how it will deliver on its broad performance target. This target is to provide the operational framework within which an advanced, competitive telecommunications sector can develop and provide consumers with the services they need at low prices.

The theme of this conference indicates the progress made from the old supposed dichotomy between control and anarchy, between a perceived requirement for a very small 's' for submission before a very large 'A' for Authority, lest anarchy prevail. It is a sign of national maturity that we can move organisations outside of the traditional constraints, putting trust in the professionalism and responsibility of those charged with setting them up and delivering services.

Establishment and functions of ODTR

The ODTR was established on 30 June under an Act passed at the end of 1996. This Act transferred to the Director the telecommunications regulatory functions of the Minister for Transport, Energy and Communications. In this context, telecommunications means radio, broadcasting and telephony. The ODTR is also the national regulatory authority, or NRA, in respect of European Union provisions for the telecommunications sector.

The regulatory functions are wide-ranging and complex. The most fundamental is that of licensing. The granting of licences, the setting of licence conditions, and the management of compliance with those conditions are major regulatory activities. We have responsibility for managing the radio spectrum, licensing the use of frequencies for radio, telephony and broadcasting. We are also responsible for licensing and managing the liberalised market for telecommunications services. We have a large range of service clients, including Telecom Éireann, Stentor, Cable and Wireless, RTÉ and the TV cable companies, radio taxis and other users of business radio.

Regulation – why independent?

Perhaps I should start by answering the question – why do we have an independent regulator? One answer: it was required under EU law, and essential in order to build a strategic alliance for Telecom Éireann. However, it is useful to look beyond this, to see why the EU and strategic investors require independent regulation.

First, for more than a decade, the telecommunications industry has been undergoing a revolution which is becoming ever more intense. Telecommunications, already embracing radio and cable, is linking up with the entertainment and information industries. The old structure in European Union countries of a state-funded monopoly providing basic telephone services to all is no longer adequate to the task of mobilising funds or for delivering services.

Competing services are needed to improve the quality and range of services and to bring prices down. Even state companies across Europe need private investment to maintain and develop their businesses.

The European Union recognised this in the 1980s and in 1984 the first Council Recommendation was published. Over the years the framework for opening EU markets to competitors of the state monopolies has been developed. The first measures covered equipment harmonisation; others provided initial ground rules to enable competitors get going. EU directives now extend to a full framework for complete liberalisation of the telecommunications market. The European Commission encountered much opposition along the way and showed much ingenuity in promoting the adoption of this framework, including an innovative use of Article 90 of the Treaty of Rome as a basis for some of its Directives.

It may be noted that, in the initial analyses of the case for liberalisation, there was significant cross-subsidisation of residential by business customers. Measures for liberalisation have been framed to introduce competition for business before residential, and for bigger telephony users before smaller ones.

As competition starts, existing operators also improve delivery and reduce prices, and the battles for market share result in larger overall markets. A quick glance at the development of the mobile phone market in Ireland up to 1994 compared with the market since then shows this clearly. The competition for the second mobile licence was announced in 1994 and this, followed by the arrival of the second mobile operator, has had a major impact. It took nearly a decade for mobile phone usage to move up to 5 per cent: since 1994 it has more than doubled, while prices have fallen significantly.

While OFTEL, the UK Regulator, has been in existence for thirteen years, liberalisation of telecommunications and the setting up of independent regulators is new in the rest of the EU. Most of the new regulators were set up in 1997. Regulation has of course existed since the beginnings of competition, but its combination in government ministries with the share holding in the incumbent operator has not been considered effective. The EU requires member states' communications ministries either to divest themselves of the incumbent operator share holding or of the regulatory function.

Private investors and telecommunications companies are willing to calculate and undertake commercial risk, but are less comfortable with political risks – an unpredictable election, a change of policy – which they cannot factor easily into their financial calculations for assessing investments. What these companies need is clarity and certainty with respect to licences and permissions. They require service delivery standards in respect of these, standards which match their own single-minded concentration on developing their businesses. Hence the need to set up dedicated independent bodies dealing with their industry, delivering the necessary services unaffected by general governmental constraints and other priorities. I may note that many incumbent operators also welcome the development of independent regulation, as they too seek to adapt their businesses to the new market conditions.

Independent regulation – why regulate?

If there is to be regulation, it should be independent. But let us consider briefly if regulation is in fact needed. Could one abolish all regulation and licensing and just let market forces operate alone? If liberalisation and competition are the keys to ensuring a better range of services and ever-decreasing prices, why not just let this happen?

The problem is that the telecommunications market has been a monopoly. The entry costs of starting completely from scratch without access to the incumbents' network are impossibly high. New players could not establish themselves without special regulation of the market, in particular ensuring access to facilities at reasonable prices in the initial stages. If there is no league, or if teams cannot get onto the pitch to play the game, it is pointless to let new players put forward their names to play.

This is an issue not merely in the telecommunications market, but in the liberalisation of utilities generally. Decades of investment in infrastructure and monopoly coverage of customers give the incumbents advantages no other players would be able to overcome without special regulation. The playing pitch is extremely bumpy. The regulatory rules are designed to enable new players into the game and provide effective competition to the incumbents. Consumers reap the benefits of lower prices, and a wider range of better services.

Sporting similes are common in the regulatory business, and the image of referee of a football match is not a bad one, in that the referee leaves the players to get on with their match, intervening only when someone breaks the rules. However, the neat image of a match lasting a fixed period with a fixed number of players per team all playing hurling or soccer or whatever, is far too static for the fast moving telecommunications industry.

Because the playing pitch is bumpy, the referee has to work hard at demolishing the bumps while the governing body is developing new rules, and new players are arriving all the time. Indeed – some new arrivals are swimmers, not football players at all! They argue that if some of the pitch were just lowered six feet and filled with water, a very interesting land and water football game could be developed for the benefit of spectators. Somebody else wants the use of the whole pitch for just five minutes every two hours, so they can land airbuses. The regulator has to be able to referee the various matches and potential plays between all these interests, representing the converging of technologies of telephone, cable and radio. These will provide an ever-greater range of services from the plain old telephone to video on demand to interactive TV and internet.

Market access is the best-known element of regulation. However, there are other very important regulatory activities, in particular managing the radio spectrum. There are many long-standing clients for radio spectrum, including business radio and broadcasting bodies, but there is also ever-increasing demand for radio spectrum for new telecommunications services. The spectrum must be managed effectively as a scarce resource, with clear, fair rules.

Regulatory rules

The rules governing the regulation of the telecommunications market are mainly set down in EU telecommunications and competition law. They are fairly complex, reflecting the nature of the industry as it liberalises. They impose a wide range of obligations on the incumbent operators, including requirements to deliver specific types of access to their networks, and transparency in pricing services to other operators.

In time, it should be possible to reduce this sector-specific regulation to sector specific and more general competition rules. Experience in other countries does not suggest that there can be a rapid fading away of regulation. In fact the opposite happens. Opening competition involves more regulation for the reasons I have described. Even in the countries which are most advanced, regulatory measures are used along with sector-specific competition rules combined with general ones, to ensure an open and fair market. What is important is that regulators have the specialised skills, and the commercial and technological information needed, to adapt their regulation to changing market conditions as required. Ireland is only at the initial stages of competition, and is just developing its regulatory framework at present.

The Irish telecommunications market

Telecommunications in Ireland improved very significantly in the 1980s and over the last decade prices have declined substantially. The recent competition for the Information Town of Ireland attracted a high level of interest, marking a growing awareness of what the future holds for this sector. At government level there is a clear recognition of the importance of preparing Ireland for the information society as evidenced by its recent adoption of the *Information Society Ireland – Strategy for Action Report*. The report outlines what is needed under five headings – awareness, infrastructure, learning, enterprise and government. It recognises the critical role that private sector investment will play, and acknowledges the importance of this new type of society, catering for all citizens in terms of equal and universal access.

However, Ireland's current position looks less glowing when set against that of other countries. Prices have come down but are still above the OECD average for both business and residential customers. New information-age technology is available for the top range of businesses, but beyond that, penetration is very limited. Even penetration of the basic telephone service, at four-fifths of Irish households, is significantly below the top performers in OECD. Internationally, we are rated twenty-third in terms of preparedness for the information society, in the third division with Spain and the Czech Republic, well behind Denmark (in third position), New Zealand (ninth) and behind Taiwan and Korea, at twenty-first and twenty-second respectively.

In 1996, the government sought some derogations from the EU timetables for liberalising the Irish telecommunications market on the grounds that Telecom Éireann would not be able to adjust quickly enough to them. The European Commission agreed to most of the requests.

The market for value-added services (that is, all services apart from real-time voice telephony) has been liberalised since 1992. Many companies now provide these services to businesses in Ireland, in competition with Telecom Éireann. Since 1 July 1997, companies may also build and use their own networks for delivery of liberalised telecommunications services, and the remainder of the derogations for Telecom Éireann run out by the year 2000. From that year, any company can sell any telephony service to anyone in Ireland or abroad, and the full provisions of EU liberalised market law will apply.

Telecom Éireann and its competitors are preparing for that date, and so too is my office. The Celtic Tiger has taken the international computer industry in its stride and it must do the same with telecommunications. It is estimated by Forfás that some 30-40,000 jobs should be created in the sector by 2010. Particularly for business, but also on social grounds, our geographical location demands that we succeed in this sector, and have available to all the most advanced range of services and continuous innovation. This requires major investment and low prices. Telecommunications growth means jobs, not alone in the industry itself, but in all sectors. Cheap, advanced communications are essential to the competitiveness of the Irish economy generally.

Role of ODTR

What is the role of the ODTR in all this? It may be useful to deal first with some misconceptions. We are not a grant-giving body like Forfás or IDA. We are not a government department like Public Enterprise. We are not responsible for telecommunications law generally.

In the context of the legislative framework created for us, our task is to provide the regulatory structure within which a competitive telecommunications sector can develop and provide consumers with cheap and advanced telecommunications services.

What we must do is provide a clear, straightforward, fair licensing system. We must provide effective market regulation and enforcement of licences, carefully adapted to market needs. It is up to the operators and investors to deliver the keenly-priced range of services consumers need, with the support of agencies such as Forfás.

Independence of the regulator

Independence is a guiding principle set down in the 1996 Act establishing the ODTR. Under the Act a wide range of regulatory functions have passed from the minister to me as director. It is a measure of how seriously the need for independent regulation is viewed by the government.

The primary guarantees of independence contained in the Act are:

- a statutory requirement to act in an independent manner, and special provisions on removal from office;

- provision for independent exercise of virtually all regulatory functions;

- provision of the right, on the part of the director, to specify and receive resource requirements;

- provision of the entitlement to the director to appoint staff to the office;

- provision for independent funding of the office by the telecommunications industry.

The relationship between these provisions is crucial to ensuring that the director is functionally, legally and financially independent. For example, an arrangement which left the office dependent on the minister or Exchequer would not be possible if the office is to develop and enjoy the full confidence of the market. On the other hand, it must be noted that the office is not a creature of the industry. It is set up under statute, its income determined by statutory instrument. This underpins the opportunity and obligation on the office to provide the regulatory service which the industry needs now. We are not competing with other government priorities for attention.

Legal discontinuity

The statutory requirement to act independently establishes a legal discontinuity between my actions as director and those of ministers who were previously responsible for the functions I now have.

Although I have taken over the on-going business of the Department of Public Enterprise in relation to transferred functions, statutory independence implies legal discontinuity. It is up to me to consider afresh what policies should be pursued. I would not discharge my obligation to act independently by just following on the past without consideration. The establishment of the ODTR marked a new beginning and a break with the past. In a number of areas, I have made changes – for example in relation to radio links application procedures for links above 1Ghz. The old procedures were geared to dealing with a small number of organisations – in particular Telecom Éireann, the mobile phone operators and the Irish Aviation Authority – and are no longer appropriate with the liberalisation of network provision to new operators.

The old procedures for radio links reflected a way of implementing policy which is not appropriate to the new competitive telecommunications market. There was much informality in submitting applications and often informal rounds of negotiation with applicants. These were helpful of course to individual applicants on a first come, first served basis, but could close off options for later ones and result in a very unclear picture as to what the policy actually was. There are large costs involved in applying under these conditions, and they can constitute an informal but quite effective deterrent to new entrants or to the introduction of new products or ideas, even by existing players. In devising its new procedures, the ODTR is operating a different model, one where the terms are clearly set out and applied simply and directly, having regard to the needs of the industry.

Accountability

Broadly speaking, there are two strands to accountability of the Director of Telecommunications Regulation. The first of these is the specific provisions on accountability in the 1996 Act: the second arises from the principles of administrative law.

The 1996 Act

The Act contains a number of requirements in respect of reporting on the activities and accounts of the office, and for seeking the consent of the Minister for Public Enterprise on specific issues.

On an annual basis, I am required by the Act to make reports to the minister and to the Houses of the Oireachtas on the performance of my office and on its financial management by way of annual accounts. The accounts will be audited by the Comptroller and Auditor General. These formal annual reports will provide a comprehensive statement on the activities undertaken and results achieved, and provide an opportunity for review and discussion of progress in the ODTR.

The Act also requires that I seek the consent of ministers in specific limited areas, for example the Minister for Public Enterprise on regulations governing the issue of wireless telegraphy licences, and of the Minister for Finance on fees for telephony licences. It also enables the issue of ministerial directions on the frequency management matters and public service requirements in relation to mobile phone licences. These provisions ensure that the operations of the ODTR in these areas do not conflict with government policy.

These provisions are the key elements of the statutory framework within which the minister and I and the relevant government departments must work. The legal obligations on all parties are quite clear, and changes have been made to reflect them.

Administrative law

Decisions taken by the ODTR have wide-ranging implications for players in the telecommunications industry. There is an obligation to ensure that decisions are taken in the context of a properly developed framework and with a full understanding of their legal and commercial impact.

All decisions made by my office must be reasoned and justified, and notified in appropriate detail to all parties concerned. This openness is a powerful stimulus to ensuring that ODTR decisions can stand up to the full rigours of in-depth analysis and scrutiny. Of course, the decision-making process must take into account the fact that genuine business secrets and certain other matters cannot be disclosed.

The telecommunications law of the EU dictates in large measure the specific powers of the regulators in member states. That law establishes certain rights for telecommunications service providers, in addition to existing rights to seek review or redress though the national courts.

EU telecommunications law requires member states to provide an appeal system. The law in Ireland implementing that obligation provides that any decision by me to refuse to grant, or to suspend or revoke a licence may, subject to judicial review:

- in the case of mobile telephony licences, be appealed to the High Court, and

- in the case of licences to provide other liberalised services be appealed to the District Court.

Consultation

An independent public body needs to listen, and explain what it is about. In my view the best way of doing this is by open consultation and transparent decision making. I am establishing a general strategy of open consultation to be undertaken before adoption of major policies. This will involve the publication of both initial consultation papers and the comments received on them. Decisions will then be taken and policies published; implementation will follow.

Our current consultation policy is limited as we have just started and all the deadlines we must meet are very tight. I intend to develop it further in 1998. This does not mean that I intend to have a heavy structure. That would delay necessary policy making for very long periods, which would be entirely inappropriate for a fast-moving industry. There will always be times when decisions are needed more rapidly than a full consultation process would allow. In keeping with the principle of independence, the judgement call on these lies with me.

Consultation is one of the ways by which we will ensure that we are fully informed of the commercial and other considerations affecting the market. We are identifying a programme of licensing and operational issues in respect of which we need to investigate and develop policies, so that our decisions are based on the best information and advice available. For example, a study on future uses of the UHF band and related issues in connection with broadcasting was commissioned in August 1997. We have also initiated work on a range of cost accounting issues in relation to Telecom Éireann. This will form the basis for many of my decisions on cross-subsidisation, prices for competitor access to the Telecom Éireann network, prices between competitors' networks and assessing general anti-competitive behaviour.

ODTR – progress to date

The principles are important, but what about the practice? The ODTR has been operating for four months, since 30 June 1997. To give you the briefest summary on major issues to date, may I just note that infrastructure liberalisation took effect on 1 July, and I am pleased to say that we succeeded in revising the licensing processes for radio links and introducing one for infrastructure within six weeks of that date. Wholesale rates for telecommunications service providers were introduced by Telecom Éireann for the first time in October.

We are engaged in further discussions on the range of accounting issues essential to ensuring a proper basis for pricing of services and separation of monopoly and non-monopoly services. Following a detailed examination of the issues, we have published a clear and unequivocal paper on voice telephony which outlined how this issue is being managed. We are also developing the terms for a mobile telephony licence competition we will run very shortly.

Shaping the organisation

It is only very recently that we have been able to give some time as a group to developing our ethos and mission. We recognise the unique opportunity we have to put in place an organisation, systems and procedures that best suit the environment within which the office operates. This environment is increasingly dynamic and driven by commercial considerations, with some planning horizons under five years as compared with fifteen to twenty years, for example in electricity and transport infrastructure investment.

We are reviewing our approaches and priorities to see how we can achieve a fully efficient and effective organisation which is focused on serving all of its service clients. Our performance delivery needs to cover rapid licensing, effective and consistent enforcement, and speedy handling of industry complaints. We have set up a series of focus groups at middle management level to ensure that longer term planning is carried forward, not as a discrete exercise separate from implementation, but as an integral part of the work of all officers.

ODTR approach

Starting from the statutory position as set out already, we have developed some practical working principles to guide our work. Some are specific to our functions, but most of these principles will govern good public sector practice under the developing Strategic Management Initiative. In the ODTR we must be mindful of the fact that, in addition to normal taxes, the industry pays directly to fund our operations. This gives us freedom from many general government constraints, freedom we must use to provide services to meet private and public sector delivery requirements while maintaining the uniquely public sector principle of equity in our ethos and in all major decisions.

These principles are:

- independence in decision making
- promotion of competition
- light-handed regulation
- consumer care
- openness and transparency
- clarity
- timeliness.

Independence in decision making

I have dealt at length with this and will make only one operational point here, which is nevertheless of critical importance. While we will provide as many opportunities as possible for all parties to make their views known, decisions will be taken independently on each case, without reference to any outside influences.

In the light of what I have already said, the importance we attach to facilitating competition is very clear. Where choices have to be made about prioritising issues, the impact on competitiveness between market players will be a key criterion.

Light-handed regulation

What is not broken does not need to be fixed. If market players can sort issues out among themselves, so much the better, so long as the settlement is not at the expense of the consumer. However, at present there are many instances where players need regulatory support. Where action is needed, I will intervene. I will have a light-handed approach, but not, let me assure you, a soft approach, and a firm hand will be used where needed.

Consumer care

For my office, consumer care is not only a matter of how we deal with our licensees, it also has wider implications. Licences are provided to enable services to be supplied. These services must be of appropriate quality. Complaints about quality in the telecommunications sector are dealt with by a number of agencies at present. However, as is evident from other sectors, quality control works when, and only when, the senior management of companies take it seriously.

I am encouraging an approach under which transparent and performance-related self-regulation would be adopted as standard in the industry. Consumer complaints should be dealt with independently of management functions. If consumer complaints are handled effectively by the industry, the ODTR can deal with complaints about systemic problems, including those noted in public information on complaints supplied by the industry itself or raised by consumer bodies such as the Director of Consumer Affairs.

Openness and transparency
I have dealt with the issues here already and will just re-emphasise the importance of an open style of management.

Clarity
Clarity is essential. We must ensure that all the decisions and actions of my office are clearly set out. This is quite a challenge given our legislative framework and the complexity of the industry. Nevertheless, we have already started with new application systems and guidelines for some key licenses.

Timeliness
Horizons are very short in the telecommunications industry. We have to be quick in responding and reaching decisions. We are determined to ensure that new players do not have long waiting periods for important decisions. We have begun to achieve results in relation to current issues, but we still have a fair amount of catching up to do, in

particular on policy development, so that we can respond to market needs. An example of this is numbering in a liberalised environment.

Conclusion

It is a great honour and also a great responsibility to be appointed to a statutory post, to have one's terms of reference set out in an Act of the Oireachtas. The challenge is enormous, in terms of establishing the ODTR, ensuring that it is independent and appropriately accountable, and also in terms of the work to be done.

I would like to finish by paying tribute to the staff of the ODTR and to those experts whom we have engaged to provide specialist services; they have responded with enthusiasm and flexibility to the tasks of developing new approaches to the key issues, also in maintaining and improving delivery of services for this most challenging and exciting office.

6

Implications of New
Organisational Structures

Michael G. Tutty
Second Secretary General, Department of Finance

Introduction

Adequate and effective arrangements for governance and accountability within the civil service and between the civil service, the political level and citizens generally are fundamental elements of a democratic system of government. I should say that governance is about the collection of rules, standards and norms that inform the behaviour of civil and public servants and politicians in conducting the business of the state with and on behalf of the public. There is a wide range of changes taking place in the civil service at present under the general umbrella of the Strategic Management Initiative (SMI) to empower and strengthen our governance and accountability arrangements. Some of these changes are simply administrative changes in the way business is conducted in the civil service. Others are more fundamental in nature and need to be underpinned by legislation. Collectively, these changes are designed to provide greater accountability and openness for the work of the civil service and to improve its performance so that it can give better service to the government and the public.

In this paper, I propose to concentrate on the governance and accountability implications of the changes now being put in place under the Public Service Management Act, 1997. But, in doing so, I must stress that the changes being implemented under the SMI constitute an integrated approach to putting in place a new civil service structure for *Delivering Better Government*, as per the title of the 1996 policy document.

To this end, and to provide the necessary legal framework for the new structure, key pieces of legislation have been enacted this year – including the Public Service Management Act, 1997, the Freedom of Information Act, 1997, and the Committees of the Houses of the Oireachtas (Compellability, Privileges and Immunities of Witnesses) Act, 1997. Summaries of the provisions of these legislative changes are attached in an appendix. The statutes enacted this year are but the latest in a series of Acts, stretching back to the 1970s, aimed at improving governance and accountability arrangements – including, *inter alia*, the Ombudsman Act, the Data Protection Act, the Ethics in Public Office Act, the amendments to the Electoral Acts, and the Comptroller and Auditor General (Amendment) Act. These Acts have all added to greater accountability and openness in the civil service. Moreover, the process of legislative change is ongoing as there are, for example, specific proposals in the government's programme to extend the remit of the Ombudsman to other parts of the public service. The current developments are, however, an integral part of the SMI process which highlighted the need to develop new structures of management.

Why a new structure? The civil service plays a central and significant role in the conduct of government business: in terms of the allocation and redistribution of resources through public expenditure and revenue; direct and indirect effects of public service employment; and the regulatory and administrative role of government. Accordingly, maintaining the highest standards in relation to management and performance in the civil service and the delivery of services are issues of major concern for all of us. A better civil service will benefit all sectors of the economy and all sections of society. I believe we can all agree that the pressures and challenges facing government today have changed very significantly in recent years, calling for more innovative approaches to solving problems and addressing our economic and social needs. These pressures and challenges arise from a greatly expanded economy, increasing economic globalisation, a relentless growth in international competitiveness, public demand for more and better services and societal changes generally, to name but a few. If the civil service is to continue to meet the needs of the country, it has to continuously adapt to being more pro-active and responsive to meeting today's challenges. In this regard, the SMI process requires a constant motivation from the government and the Oireachtas, commitment and effort from civil and public servants at all levels and a willingness by all concerned to accept and implement change in the conduct of government business.

A commitment to a continuous process of modernisation underpins the announcements made by the Taoiseach in Dublin Castle on 29 July. In particular, the establishment of a high-level Implementation Group of Secretaries General, charged with responsibility for driving forward the process of change in the civil service, will ensure that the momentum of change is accelerated over the months ahead. In carrying forward the needed changes, senior management in the civil service, in common with all sides at a political level, are committed to maintaining the traditional strengths and values of the Irish public service: commitment to national goals, high standards of propriety and impartiality and a willingness to adapt and respond positively to challenges. The change process is emphatically not an attempt to impose a new model of public administration from the UK, New Zealand or any other country. The focus is on the real needs of citizens and users of the public services and the importance of adjusting to actual circumstances and conditions in Ireland. The process is – most emphatically – not about actualising some abstract or theoretical concepts of public services. The programme of change is rooted in the institutions, traditions and organisations of the Irish civil service itself.

I will review briefly the existing accountability arrangements before going on to outline the changes which are being introduced and considering the implications of these for how the civil service is managed.

Constitutional provisions

Article 28 of the constitution, Bunreacht na hÉireann, provides the basis in primary law on which the relationship between the government, individual ministers, government departments and the Oireachtas is framed. The key relevant provisions are as follows:

Article 28.4.2°   The Government shall meet and act as a collective authority, and shall be collectively responsible for the Departments of State administered by the members of the Government.

Article 28.12   The following matters shall be regulated in accordance with law, namely, the organisation of, and distribution of business amongst, Departments of State, the designation of members of the Government to be the Ministers in charge of the said Departments, the discharge of the functions of the office of a member of the Government during his temporary absence or incapacity, and the remuneration of the members of the Government.

Of particular importance to the process of establishing the proposed new management structure in the civil service are the words '...administered...' in Article 28.4.2°, and '...in charge of...' in Article 28.12. The use of these terms in the Constitution means that only a member of the government can be 'in charge of' a department of state under Article 28.4.2°.

However, the constitutional provisions do not mean that a minister is inhibited from assigning authority and responsibility in respect of the 'management' of some or all of the functions of a department of state to a secretary of a department or another civil servant. Similarly, *ministerial* accountability for the work of departments does not prevent the enactment of legislation to provide in law for a mechanism of accountability for civil servants under the minister.

Existing accountability structures for civil servants

The statutory basis for the accountability of civil servants derives from the Ministers and Secretaries Acts, 1924-1995, the Civil Service Regulation Act, 1956, the Comptroller and Auditor General (Amendment) Act, 1993 and some other relevant legislation.

Under these provisions, secretaries are appointed by the government on the recommendation of relevant ministers as 'principal officers' of their departments. Other officers are appointed by their minister with the sanction of the Minister for Finance. Secretaries and other general civil servants are accountable to the government and to their individual ministers. Secretaries are also accountable, as accounting officers, to the Public Accounts Committee of Dáil Éireann.

The Minister for Finance is responsible for the regulation and control of the civil service, their classification, numbers and remuneration and terms and conditions of service, promotion and discipline. Only the government has had the authority to dismiss established civil servants.

Changes in structures of governance and accountability

The practical changes now being implemented in the administration of central government are intended, in the first instance, to improve the internal management of the civil service. Therefore, *prima facie*, their immediate impact will mainly be on civil servants and ministers. But the consequences of these changes are intended to go well beyond the confines of government departments and offices. The changes are designed to ensure greater efficiency and effectiveness across all branches of the public service in order to ensure quality in the delivery of services. Business and the general public will benefit from this, firstly as users and as consumers of public services, and secondly, as taxpayers who finance the public expenditure needed to ensure the delivery of public services.

While the central emphasis in the current phase of the SMI process is on comprehensive structural change through the creation of a new management structure for the civil service by means of the Public Service Management Act 1997, there are parallel developments in the areas of human resource management, information technology, auditing, government accounting and financial management. We recognise also that, as the process evolves, increased attention will need to be directed towards the more 'cultural' dimension of organisational change.

In identifying the central organisational and structural issues within the SMI process, previous proposals for change have been drawn on. Even a cursory knowledge of the period of the Devlin Report in the 1970s, or the policy priorities identified in the context of the White Paper *Serving the Country Better* published in the mid-1980s, will reveal the same fundamental issues as are being addressed by the SMI.

As *Delivering Better Government* puts it (page 22):

> It has long been recognised that the existing structures and reporting systems promote a risk-averse environment where taking personal responsibility is not encouraged and, equally, where innovative approaches to service delivery have not been developed.

Underpinning this is the conviction that long-standing practice has tended to concentrate too much on the responsibility of the ministers, leaving the accountability of civil servants unclear.

The role of civil servants under the law, including that of departmental secretaries, has not been adequately addressed in legislation up to now. The Ministers and Secretaries Acts do not set out in detail the form of authority and responsibility which may be exercised by officials of departments in conducting public service business. This situation gave rise over time to a tendency for decisions to be taken at too high a level and for authority to become unduly centralised which, in turn, resulted in structures which did not always ensure optimal levels of efficiency and effectiveness.

The group of secretaries responsible for the report on which *Delivering Better Government* was based identified a causal connection between the legal basis for the organisation of the public service and interpretations of the respective roles of ministers and civil servants. Contemporary legal opinion on the degree of potential organisational flexibility under existing legislation suggested a less restrictive statutory framework than traditionally understood. However, it became increasingly clear that the Ministers and Secretaries Acts provided an insufficient legislative foundation to accommodate the changes required in the structure of civil service management within the existing constitutional parameters.

Accordingly, a central proposal put to government concerned the need to amend and update the existing law. Support for such measures came from all parties represented in the Oireachtas and the report and final stages of the Public Service Management Bill were unopposed in both Dáil Éireann and Seanad Éireann. Discussions among departmental secretaries and at networks of assistant secretaries and principals indicated wide support within the civil service itself for the thrust of these changes.

Public Service Management Act, 1997

Safeguarding the position of ministers
In devising the Public Service Management Act, 1997 in the light of the existing constitutional and statutory provisions, it was decided that a wholesale repeal and replacement of existing legislation was neither feasible nor necessary.

As I have already indicated, the role and status of ministers 'in charge' of departments and 'responsible' to Dáil Éireann are set out in the Constitution. Constitutional change was not seen as necessary to bring about the desirable changes in the accountability and responsibility structures for civil servants. Therefore, Section 3 of the Public Service Management Act, 1997 reaffirms that, notwithstanding any assignment of functions in the Act, a minister of the government is in charge of his or her department and is responsible for the administration of that department as provided for in the Constitution and the Ministers and Secretaries Acts, 1924 to 1995.

The Public Service Management Act, 1997 does not repeal the Ministers and Secretaries Act, 1924; it makes relatively minor amendments to that Act and creates new mechanisms for the accountability of civil servants, without diminishing the role and responsibility of ministers. The new management structure created by the Act functions 'under the Minister' and provides a number of specific safeguards which maintain the unique authority of ministers in relation to policy, the allocation of resources and their responsibility to Dáil Éireann. The Act differentiates between these constitutional functions of the minister and the assignment of authority, responsibility and accountability for carrying out duties appropriate to departments and certain other offices[1] (specified in the Schedule to the Act).

An additional safeguard of the position of ministers is Section 7 of the Act which empowers a minister to give directions in writing to a secretary of a department of state (now renamed secretary general) for any of the functions performed by the secretary general. The purpose of this provision is to ensure that the provisions of the Act do not place any restrictions on ministers in exercising ultimate authority in the administration of departments for which they are responsible to Dáil Éireann.

In including this provision, it was not envisaged that the issuing of written directions would form part of the 'normal' relationship between a minister and his/her secretary general. Indeed, the need to resort to a written direction should arise only in relation to unusual, unforeseen and infrequent developments in the work of the department. It was necessary, nevertheless, to ensure that there is no possible ambiguity with respect to the power of the minister to issue such directions to secretaries general.

However, it was considered necessary to exclude from such directions matters relating to the management of appointments, discipline, performance and dismissals which are being assigned to the secretary general under the Act. If these matters were included it could potentially dilute the authority of the secretary general in relation to staff management.

New accountability structures for civil servants
While the accountability structures relating to the political sphere are unchanged, the existing organisational arrangements for civil servants are being made more transparent and effective in the following ways:

- the accountability of secretaries general of departments to the relevant minister is put on a statutory basis;

- the accountability of secretaries general is now specified as being in respect of the exercise of authority and responsibility in relation to duties set out in the Act, subject to the determination of matters of policy by the minister or the government, including

  - managing the day-to-day business of the department
  - implementing government policies appropriate to the department
  - monitoring government policies that affect the department
  - delivering outputs as determined with the minister
  - preparing and submitting to the minister a strategy statement in respect of the department
  - providing progress reports to the minister on implementation of the strategy statement
  - providing advice to the minister
  - ensuring proper use of resources and the provision of cost-effective public services
  - assigning duties to other officers down through the department;

- officers who have been assigned functions are now being made accountable, in statute, to their secretary general and to their line manager as appropriate;

- secretaries general, or other designated officers, must now appear before Oireachtas committees when requested to do so in relation to the strategy statement for the department;

- under the Committees of the Houses of the Oireachtas (Compellability, Privileges and Immunities of Witnesses) Act, 1997, all civil servants may be compelled to appear before an Oireachtas committee with power to send for persons or papers and, in such circumstances, may be granted privilege and immunity in relation to evidence given (in such cases civil servants may not comment on the merits of government policy);

- civil servants assigned to cross-departmental groups may now be made accountable for the utilisation of related financial resources with the agreement of, and in a manner to be specified by, the Minister for Finance;

- subject to amendments to other legislation and consultation with staff, secretaries general will exercise authority in relation to appointments, performance, discipline and dismissal of all civil servants below the grade of principal or its equivalent;

- authority in relation to appointments, performance and discipline – but not dismissal – of all civil servants below the grade of principal or its equivalent may be assigned by the secretary general to other grades of civil servant;

- officers assigned duties will be directly accountable to the secretary general or other superior officers for the achievement of objectives and the delivery of specified outputs.

Freedom of Information Act

The greater transparency and openness being created by the implementation of the Freedom of Information Act will generate more confidence in the system of governance as a whole. Client relationships with the civil service will improve significantly as individuals gain the reassurance of having access to records, because people will know that their cases are dealt with fairly and impartially. A culture of openness in public administration will itself encourage quality and public services will become more efficient and effective. Freedom of information will also ensure that the highest standards are maintained in government agencies in relation to accuracy and objective record keeping. The citizen will, in effect, 'own' the official information on his or her particular case, which the public services possess. All of these factors will give added impetus to the process of change and, indirectly, assist the transition to the new structures of management and accountability in the civil service.

Implementation of organisational changes

Strategy Statements
Arising from the commencement of the Public Service Management Act on 1 September 1997, the various tiers of governance – the government itself, individual ministers and secretaries general of departments – are required to undertake a number of specified actions.

The key function is the preparation of strategy statements. Specifically, secretaries general of departments are required to prepare strategy statements and submit them to their ministers within six months – that is by March 1998. The government will soon issue directions regarding the form and manner in which these strategy statements are to be prepared. Ministers must approve the strategy statements, with or without amendment. They are then required to ensure that a copy of the strategy statement is laid before each house of the Oireachtas *not later than sixty days after the strategy statement has been approved.* The Taoiseach has indicated that this must occur, in the first instance, no later than 1 May next. A new strategy statement must be prepared within six months of the appointment of a new minister or three years after the previous statement.

It is envisaged that strategy statements will set out the key objectives, outputs and related strategies of the department, including the use of resources. They will reflect policies or targets being pursued consistent with the government's programme – *An Action Programme for the Millennium* – as well as the on-going business of the department. They will incorporate an indication of how departments will pursue the achievement of policy objectives and the practical actions of departmental management needed to achieve them. These statements will also need to indicate how the approach to the individual policy objectives fits into the overall business of the department and what arrangements and steps are being taken in relation to the overall utilisation and deployment of resources. In this way the strategy statements will provide managers within the civil service, ministers and the government, the houses of the Oireachtas and citizens generally with a clear and comprehensive framework within which arrangements for the accountability of secretaries general to their ministers will be structured.

Assignment of authority, responsibility and accountability
Secretaries general will also be required to prepare an '*outline*' of how specific elements of responsibilities are to be assigned to other civil servants or grades within their departments and then to proceed with appropriate assignments.

The key purpose of the outline is to ensure that 'the functions performed on behalf of the Minister ... are performed by an appropriate officer, or an officer of an appropriate grade or rank'. The outline will facilitate the association of individual civil servants, ranks or grades of officers given responsibility for particular functions assigned by the secretary general with the specific tasks and duties required to undertake those functions; and make it easier to relate the delivery of particular outputs and the discharge of functions or duties to the resources available for those areas within a department.

Based on this outline, the secretary general will assign responsibility for the performance of functions down through the department. This will include responsibility for providing policy advice in particular areas, achieving specified outputs, assuming responsibility for particular statutory schemes or programmes or for the delivery of quality services, ensuring value for money and performing, on behalf of the secretary general, functions in respect of appointments, performance and discipline of personnel, but not dismissals.

The secretary general may designate appropriate officers to appear before a committee of either house of the Oireachtas in relation to the

department's strategy statement where the relevant responsibility for
the performance of functions has been assigned to those officers.

Building on existing best practice
The provisions in relation to preparing strategy statements and
delegating functions to appropriate officers are not new concepts in
the civil service. The new legislative provisions simply bring a degree
of formality to earlier practice in these areas and ensure that best
practice is spread throughout the civil service.

Strategy statements have already been prepared under the SMI,
notably those prepared and published by each department in the past
year.   These will now have to be expanded and made more specific
in line with the requirements of the 1997 Act.

Under the SMI, departments have been using their statements of
strategy internally to spell out how the work of individual divisions,
work units or teams feeds into the overall strategy and what specific
outputs are to be delivered.   This internal process has taken different
forms and goes under different names – e.g. business plans, work
programmes, action programmes – but it provides the foundations on
which the assignment of functions under the 1997 Act can be built.

Overall, the new arrangements will give much greater clarity at all
levels of the civil service on what is the specific goal of each person's
work assignment and how it fits in with the overall goals of the
department and minister.

Performance Management System
Overall, therefore, the Act provides for a process by which strategic
objectives are set and reviewed regularly and inform the day-to-day
work of departments and their achievement is monitored. An effective
performance management system is clearly central to this process.
Performance management is a means of managing and developing
individual performance, in line with corporate objectives, to deliver
improved performance for the organisation as a whole.

A new performance management system for the civil service is in the final stage of design and development following extensive consultations with management, staff and the civil service group of unions. A staff survey carried out as part of these consultations shows that a majority of staff would welcome 'good practice' performance management set in the context of departments' overall objectives and involving:

- regular performance review;

- focus on development and improvement;

- reviews taking into account how jobs were done and what was achieved; and

- provision for upward feedback.

However, the survey also indicates that there is a lack of awareness of managerial responsibility and accountability throughout the organisations.

The successful introduction of an effective performance management system requires that there is a clear description of job and role requirements in terms of results to be achieved and the related performance measures and the skills, knowledge, and competencies needed to do the job. In that latter regard, performance management must be linked to and inform other HRM processes in the organisation i.e. planning, training and career development. There is also a need to focus on developing managerial capability. This focus on managerial aspects of roles is, of course, a pre-requisite to the effective implementation of the Public Service Management Act.

Taken together, the Public Service Management Act and the performance management process will provide a firm foundation for developing a more results-orientated and accountable civil service. Given the importance of the civil service in the conduct of government business, I believe we would all agree that improved levels of accountability and transparency are essential and that the workings of the service are open and can stand up to public scrutiny.

Cross-departmental arrangements

I would now like to turn to Section 12 of the Public Service Management Act, 1997, which is a major legislative innovation providing for the assignment of responsibility for cross-departmental matters. This arises from a specific recommendation in the *Delivering Better Government* report. The report argued that the existing structure of the civil service is not well geared to understanding, developing and managing the linked activities and processes needed to address issues of policy and execution which cut across a variety of departments and offices. The work of individual departments tends to be determined by sectoral and functional demands. Experience suggests that departments have 'limited structures for consultation, coordination and cooperation' and that 'the current system rewards territorial protection at the expense of active cooperation to achieve results'.

Cross-departmental groups – such as the tax strategy group and the task-force on long term unemployment – have stimulated more integrated policy approaches in the relevant areas but it has long been clear that many issues of cross-departmental concern would require a more structured and formal approach. Policy matters which would benefit from such an approach were identified in *Delivering Better Government* including:

- child care
- drugs
- employment
- competitiveness
- unemployment and social exclusion
- financial services
- local development.

The Public Service Management Act empowers ministers or ministers of state, jointly with their counterparts in one or more other departments, to assign responsibility to civil servants for the performance of functions relating to both or all of the departments concerned. The ministers continue to have the right to perform the functions concurrently. A specific provision is made in the Act for consultation with the secretaries general of the departments involved.

In framing the legislation, it was recognised that the issue of accountability is of central importance. To whom are civil servants assigned responsibilities in respect of cross-departmental groups ultimately accountable? To their parent department or office? Or to the head or chairman of the cross-departmental group? The advisory group – established to advise the Minister for Finance on the legislation – recognised that, in practical terms, the matter of accountability is inseparable from the specifics of the remit, tasks and objectives of the cross-departmental group in each case.

Accordingly, Subsection 12 (4) provides that orders assigning responsibilities to civil servants will specify to whom they shall be accountable. In addition, it was recognised that special arrangements might have to apply in relation to the disbursement of public funds by cross-departmental groups. So the legislation also provides that the Minister for Finance will have authority for specifying 'the manner of accountability' for responsibilities that involve the use of financial resources.

Human Resource Management
There is one aspect of the overall change programme which warrants mention in the context of the new structures provided for in the Public Service Management Act, that is, the management of the staff resources of the civil service. A consistent criticism of the civil service, both within the system and from outside commentators, has been that sufficient priority has not been given to human resource management. This was – to some extent – a failing common to all large organisations, whether private sector or public sector.

Underlying the SMI – and the change programme set out in *Delivering Better Government* – is a recognition of the need for a more flexible approach to managing staff resources so that staff can be deployed to best effect in meeting the changing needs and demands of today's environment, can have the opportunity to use their skills and potential in the most creative and satisfying ways, and where the most productive individuals receive rewards commensurate with their performance. In addition to performance management, every significant aspect of HR management is being looked at in the context of the modernisation process: recruitment (including atypical recruitment), training and development, probation, promotion, multiple grade structures, gender-related issues and terms of employment.

In relation to the latter, at present civil servants are appointed by ministers and hold office 'at the will and pleasure' of the government. Subject to appropriate safeguards and to natural justice and to full discussion and consultation with staff interests on the changes, powers in relation to the appointment, performance, discipline and dismissal of staff below the grade of principal or its equivalent will now be vested in secretaries general under Section 4(1)(h) of the Public Service Management Act. This change is in keeping with the formal assignment of responsibility to secretaries general for management of departments. It also brings the civil service into line with practices elsewhere.

Some issues arising from the new arrangements

The Public Service Management Act is the most fundamental statutory change in the organisation of the business of the public service since the original Ministers and Secretaries Act of 1924. Given the broad sweep of change arising from this legislation and other SMI-related initiatives, there are bound to be questions asked and criticisms levelled at the particular changes being made. This is both inevitable and positive. All levels within the civil service are affected by the process of change and development. It is entirely reasonable that civil servants should try to tease out the various consequences and nuances of the changes being made, either individually or through their unions and staff associations. Equally, the process of change itself must involve dialogue and partnership if it is to achieve the goals of the SMI.

Delivering Better Government identified five communication and consultation processes:

- at the political level, including both government and opposition;
- between government and the civil service;
- between the civil service and its customers and clients;
- at the senior levels of the civil service; and
- between all levels within the civil service through direct involvement and through consultation with trade unions and associations.

Progress on all five fronts has been made, although the extent of the direct involvement in the process has been uneven. The consultation and participation structures to be put in place under *Partnership 2000* will redress this shortcoming. These structures, which are currently the subject of discussions with the trade unions, will provide for a range of mechanisms to facilitate and encourage consultation on and participation in the change process at the level of each department. Significantly, verified progress to a satisfactory level in implementing the *Delivering Better Government* programme will be a prerequisite to the payment of the 2 per cent available under the local-level negotiation clause of the *Partnership 2000* pay agreement.

One criticism which has been made of the Public Service Management Act is that it conveys a perception of 'distancing' the minister from the day-to-day business of his/her department, in effect imposing the secretary general in place of the minister as a virtually autonomous general manager of the department. This is, in fact, a misconception. Section 3 of the Act states unequivocally that the minister is 'responsible for the performance of functions that are assigned to the Department' in accordance with the Ministers and Secretaries Acts. Every duty subsequently assigned to the secretary general under Section 4 is under the authority of the minister and subject to the determination of policy by the minister or the government. The integral role of the minister is further specified in

Section 6 which provides that the secretary general shall be 'accountable to the Minister ... in carrying out the duties or functions' assigned under Section 4. These arrangements preserve the chain of authority to the minister while at the same time creating a clear statutory basis for the exercise of managerial authority by the secretary general.

In this regard, the departmental strategy statement provides an essential management tool. Secretaries general have responsibility for preparing strategy statements but the minister can refuse to approve them, can amend them or intervene through directions in writing. Rather than creating the impression of a 'semi-detached authority', as at least one commentator has suggested, these ministerial prerogatives integrate the minister in the composition of the objectives, outputs and strategies of the department whether or not powers of amendment or direction are actually used. In effect, the minister is clearly in charge of the department.

A related criticism is that the Act enables a minister to be in charge when things go right and a civil servant in charge when things go wrong. Again, this was not part of the thinking underpinning the legislation. On the contrary, by clarifying roles and responsibilities in the new management structure, the effect of the Act is more likely to focus attention on the efficiency and effectiveness of high quality management at all levels across the civil service. There is no question of any aspect of the Act being used intentionally as a means of 'passing the buck' to civil servants. Ministers are politically accountable for their departments. If something goes wrong the Opposition and the media will demand explanations from the minister. Where civil servants have been assigned responsibilities, appropriate mechanisms of accountability will be devised but they will not be asked to account for matters over which they exercise no authority.

A further issue has been raised in relation to Section 4(1)(h) of the Act under which secretaries general are assigned authority for managing all matters relating to appointments, performance, discipline and dismissal of civil servants below the grade of principal or its equivalent, thereby creating different arrangements for principals and higher grades as opposed to other grades. Criticism of this is based on an assumption that the position and status of these other grades are being diminished relative to principals and higher grades. No such diminution was envisaged in the preparation of the legislation. Nor is there any intention of introducing procedures for any grade of officer below the level of principal without full discussion and consultation with the trade unions and staff associations. Moreover, there is no reason why the new arrangements in this regard should interfere with the working relationships between individual grades or between ministers and civil servants at any level. Changes affecting discipline and dismissals will not be made effective until the scheme of changes proposed to the Civil Service Regulation Act 1956 is put in place. Guarantees of consultation in relation to changes in the 1956 Act have been given.

There are many other issues which could be raised in relation to the governance and accountability implications of the new organisational structures. I am sure that Seán O Ríordáin will address some of them in his paper and I look forward to a discussion on these issues at this conference.

Appendix
Summary of Recent Legislative Provisions

The Public Service Management Act, 1997

- This Act introduces a statutory basis for the creation of a new management structure for the civil service.

- The purpose is to enhance the management, effectiveness and transparency of operations of departments and offices and to put in place a mechanism for increased accountability of civil servants. At the same time the discretion of ministers in charge of departments of state for the administration of their departments is virtually unchanged and the collective responsibility of the government to Dáil Éireann is preserved.

- The Act provides for the replacement of the title 'Secretary' by the new title of 'Secretary General'. In addition, it provides that managerial responsibility for the Department be assigned to the secretary general and, for offices included in the schedule, to the 'Head' of that office. It also defines the 'outputs' of a department or office.

- Under the new management structure, the Act provides that specified tasks will be assigned to secretaries general in accordance with various categories set out in the government's policy statement *Delivering Better Government.*

- The secretary general will be given formal responsibility, under the minister, for the day-to-day management of the department. This will involve implementing and monitoring policies and delivering the goods and services of the department to its customers and clients.

- Other functions include giving advice to the minister in relation to the wider concerns of his or her department, making arrangements in relation to cross-departmental matters, examining and developing means to improve the provision of cost-effective services and ensuring that the department's resources are used appropriately and with respect to value for money.

- Subject to existing legislation, secretaries general will have responsibility for appointments, performance, discipline and dismissal in relation to staff below the level of principal or its equivalent. These responsibilities will be exercised in addition to the functions which a secretary normally exercises at present in the routine management of all staff in his or her department.

- Each secretary general will be required to prepare a strategy statement setting out the specific objectives, outputs and strategies of the department. This will then be submitted to the minister who may amend it.

- The approved statement will be made available to the public through the Oireachtas within a specified time limit. Heads of scheduled offices will generally follow a similar procedure – with adjustments for those offices which are headed by independent office-holders. Provision is also made for regular updating and revising of these statements.

- It is intended that only those strategy statements laid before the Oireachtas will be on the public record. All other versions will be confidential documents for five years.

- Ministers retain a power of direction (other than in relation to dismissals of staff below principal) to ensure that, in cases of disagreement, the minister's instructions will be followed.

- The secretary general will be accountable to the minister in respect of the functions assigned and, in certain circumstances, will be required to appear before Oireachtas committees.

- The Act provides for formal assignment, by the secretary general, of specified tasks, analogous to his or her responsibilities, to other officers or grades of officer within departments. This arrangement is intended to ensure that staff at various levels in each department have a clear idea of what is expected of them.

- The Act also creates a statutory basis for the appointment of special advisers and for the assignment of responsibility for matters which cross-departmental boundaries. At present, only ministers are corporations sole which allows them to sue and be sued as corporate entities rather than as individuals. The Act provides a mechanism which would allow certain public offices to become corporations sole.

- A provision to allow for the creation of executive agencies by order of the government was part of the original scheme of the Bill. Subject to the resolution of technical issues in relation to the structure and design of such provisions, the government will consider introducing them as part of future legislation on public service management.

- The Act was brought into operation by ministerial order on 1 September 1997.

The Committees of the Houses of the Oireachtas (Compellability, Privileges and Immunities of Witnesses) Act, 1997

• Under Article 15.13 of the Constitution, TDs and Senators have absolute privilege in respect of utterances in either house and since 1976 this has been extended by legislation to committee meetings.

• Witnesses appearing before such committees have only 'qualified privilege': this does not prevent legal action being taken but it allows a defence against libel or slander unless it can be proven that a witness was actuated by a motive not connected with the privilege, e.g. ill will or spite. The risk of legal action with attendant costs, even where a good defence exists, presents a serious hazard to any witness. Qualified privilege does not extend to other legal actions which could create liability for damages, e.g. breaches of confidentiality, breach of duty or care.

• The new Act confers on Oireachtas committees, whose terms of reference include provision for the calling of persons and papers, statutory power to compel the attendance and cooperation of witnesses and the furnishing of documents. It also confers High Court privilege (virtually identical to the absolute privilege of members of Dáil Éireann or Seanad Éireann) on all persons directed to give evidence or present documents to such committees. These two elements are essential to the Act; those compelled to answer questions must be given protection from any adverse legal consequences of complete responses.

• Issue-specific legislation has been used twice in the past to confer absolute privilege for inquiries:

  – the Committee of Public Accounts of Dáil Éireann (Privilege and Procedure) Act, 1970 for the investigation of the arms crisis;

  – The Select Committee on Legislation and Security of Dáil Éireann (Privilege and Immunity) Act, 1994 for the investigation of the circumstances leading to the fall of the Fianna Fáil-Labour government.

- The Act provides that Dáil Éireann or Seanad Éireann will determine individually or jointly, in framing orders of reference for existing or new committees, whether they are to have the specific powers to send for persons or papers which would bring the compellability and privilege powers into effect.

- The Act allows for the creation (by the Committee on Procedures and Privilege of either house) of a sub-committee on compellability to determine when the powers should be brought into effect.

- In keeping with convention, the President and members of the judiciary are exempt from the legislation. Virtually every other citizen is compellable: members of the public, Taoiseach, Tánaiste, ministers, ministers of state and officials: a partial restriction applies to civil servants, gardaí and members of the defence forces who may not question or express comments on the merits (or the merits of the objectives) of government policies.

- Compellability of the Attorney General is limited to the general administration of his office before the Public Accounts Committee; the Attorney General is not compellable in his roles as legal advisor to the government or as defender of the public interest.

- The Director of Public Prosecutions is compellable before the Public Accounts Committee for the general administration of his office and statistics published in a report.

- Compellability is restricted in relation to evidence or documents likely to prejudice:
  - cabinet confidentiality
  - matters *sub judice*
  - state security and relations with other states
  - criminal matters
  - tax liability assessment.

- Witnesses may also inform a committee if they believe a direction falls within categories for which the High Court would grant privilege (e.g. self-incrimination, marital privacy and sacerdotal confidentiality).

- If a committee wishes to proceed with questioning a witness who gives such an opinion, the committee may seek a determination by the High Court as to whether a direction falls within such a category.

- The Act has been signed by Uachtarán na hÉireann and may be brought into effect with respect to a committee of either house of the Oireachtas by means of a resolution of that house.

The Freedom of Information Act, 1997

- The Freedom of Information Act, 1997 was signed by the President in April 1997 and comes into operation with effect from 21 April 1998.

- The Freedom of Information Act gives individual citizens a legal entitlement to have access to official information kept on them by the state. The intention of the Act is to ensure that members of the public may exercise this 'right to know' to the greatest extent possible consistent with the public interest and legitimate rights to privacy.

- By providing the citizen with a statutory right of access to official information the law fundamentally changes the nature of the relationship between the citizen and the state. It alters the balance of power between institutions of the state and individuals to give greater advantage to the citizen.

- Up to now, the institutions of the state maintained the principle of confidentiality in relation to the business of government; until 1972, the state successfully maintained the position that ministers could not be compelled by court order to produce official documents for inspection. Even today, costly, formal and time-consuming legal processes are required to access some forms of official information. Freedom of Information changes this.

- The Freedom of Information Act will bring about the following key changes:

- there will now be a statutory right to official information based on a presumption of openness;
- necessary exemptions will be subject to an overall public interest test;
- a public register of information and guidelines to be used in decision making by government bodies will come into play;
- there will be a legal obligation on officials to help citizens requesting information to identify and find what they need to know;
- there will be an onus on those who hold information to justify any refusal to disclose such information;
- there will be a powerful independent appeals system to resolve disputes between citizens and public bodies promptly and without undue expense.

• A central policy unit has been established in the Department of Finance to lead the implementation process and provide ongoing advice and support to public bodies. It will

- chair the inter-departmental working group on Freedom of Information which monitors and coordinates policies and approaches to implementation;
- provide for the establishment of the Office of the Information Commissioner (Mr Kevin Murphy, Ombudsman);
- address information management and training issues arising from Freedom of Information;
- develop expert knowledge on the form and content of publications required under sections 15 and 16 (information on records held; means of access; etc.) of the Act.

• The objectives of the Freedom of Information Act include the following:

- greater transparency in policy making will generate more confidence in the system of governance as a whole;
- client relationships with government bodies will improve as individuals gain the reassurance of having access to records; people will know that their cases are dealt with fairly and impartially.

– an administrative culture which promotes openness rather than unnecessary secrecy will develop across the public services;
– openness will itself encourage quality; our public services will become more efficient and effective;
– freedom of information legislation will ensure that the highest standards are maintained in government agencies in relation to accuracy and objective record keeping;
– the citizen will be made central to the democratic process because the citizen will, in effect, 'own' the official information on his or her particular case, which the public services possess.

Note

1. To avoid repetition, reference will be made in the rest of this paper only to departments and secretaries general of departments, though the Act applies equally to the scheduled offices and heads of those offices.

7

Implications of New Organisational Structures
– A Trade Union Perspective

Seán O Ríordáin

Association of Higher Civil Servants

Introduction

The theme of this session is the Governance and Accountability Implications of New Organisational Structures, and I have been asked to address it from a trade union perspective, particularly in the light of the Strategic Management Initiative (SMI) and the Public Service Management Act.

The trade union perspective I bring is that of the Association of Higher Civil Servants (AHCS). The Association has, since 1992, when it was neither popular nor profitable, advocated strategic change in the civil service. The adoption of a strategic management approach demands cross-department co-ordination, greater delegation, better financial and human resource management, more openness and transparency, and a focus on a quality service to the public. These were all at the heart of the AHCS proposals and are now crucial to the SMI. Most of our proposals have been adopted. Some have not and I will return to these later. We support strategic management, but we are not afraid to ask the awkward question where it is necessary to do so.

Power Structures

I want to touch briefly on structures of power and responsibility in the civil service. The Constitution is unambiguously clear. It is members of the government who are both in charge of the departments of state and who are collectively responsible to Dáil Éireann for departments of state administered by them.

The Public Service Management Act provides that, subject to the determination of matters of policy by the minister, the secretary general shall have the authority, responsibility and accountability for managing the department. The secretary general is also responsible for assigning functions to officers or grades.

The difference between policy and management is not defined in the Act and, while there is provision for the minister to give directions to the secretary general, there is no direct provision for the minister giving directions to any other civil servant.

The grades we represent in the AHCS regularly deal on a one-to-one basis with ministers. They do so on issues of both policy and management against a background where government could not function properly if everything had to be routed through secretaries general. In the real world they may do so on occasion in situations of some divergence of views between ministers and secretaries general. The legal advice the Association has received is that members of the civil service must, in principle, accept directions from the secretary general and should particularly do so if those matters are referred to in Section 4 of the Public Service Management Act, e.g. management issues. Civil servants if they are wise will not attempt to adjudicate between matters of conflicting direction from the minister and the secretary general but, if in doubt, we are advised that they should in law follow directions from the secretary general to whom they are accountable.

Under the old model we all knew who the boss was. Under the new model in which the secretary general may appoint, promote, discipline and dismiss – who is the real boss? From a trade union perspective, are we to be faced when we make representations to ministers with the response that these are matters of management for which ministers are no longer responsible? Power is a concept perceived from differing perspectives. If, over time, the perceived perspective at senior level in the civil service is that power has shifted, will this affect the actual exercise of power?

This is not an academic point. The issue of who is in charge in a democracy is of vital importance. Irrespective, however, of any divergence between legal responsibility for policy and management, I tend to believe that the average man or woman on the Ballyfermot omnibus will in the first instance blame the minister if something serious goes wrong, whether in policy or management. That is not to say that the minister will not blame the civil service! And, if the blame is justified, civil servants should properly be accountable.

A Board Structure

The recent tribunals of inquiry have resulted in an unprecedented focus on openness, transparency and accountability in decision making. And yet, if we are to look for a list of decisions taken by any department of state on a yearly basis there would be great difficulty in getting such a list. By comparison, every decision of government, formal or informal, is recorded and in time the government agenda, the memoranda and counter memoranda and the book of minutes recording government decisions are passed to the National Archives.

The government functions in a board type of structure and the view of our association is that, for maximum effectiveness, departments should also function more as a board. We had envisaged the minister, in effect, being an executive chairperson, the secretary general being the chief executive and the various senior functional heads acting as directors. We also envisaged a situation where important decisions would, where possible, be taken within that structure after open discussion and consideration of any appropriate papers or submissions.

The advantage of a board structure is self-evident. If any of you, or indeed the government itself, were setting up a new organisation tomorrow, power would not be divided on the basis of responsibility for policy being given to one person and management to another. The board structure is what would be used. We believe that even within the confines of the Public Service Management Act, there should be guidelines drawn up for a board type structure. This would be a very practical and positive development that would better reflect the constitutional relationship of ministers to the administration of departments.

Freedom of Information

While we are talking about openness and transparency, I would like to say something briefly about the Freedom of Information Act. There is no doubt but that the requirements of the Act and the potential focus of increased scrutiny on decision making will bring home the need to ensure not alone that justice is done but that it is seen to be done. We have supported freedom of information for years and we welcome the Act. I hope, however, that it does not lead to a change in culture under which civil servants will be less than willing to give honest advice, or will feel that everything has to be put on paper in endless self-justification. Quite apart from the public import, the Act will also be used in the context of access to personnel records, and we will have to see where that leads.

There is one area of some regret for our association in this context. We believe that the Act should have included what is commonly called a 'whistleblower' provision. We had looked for this and a form of it was included in the original draft published but it was left out in the final Act. We still believe that public interest would be served by a mechanism which would enable public servants to raise – with an ombudsman type person but not in the media – possible issues of illegality or serious maladministration in a manner which does not leave them open to criminal or administrative sanction. While such a provision might reasonably be used in only truly exceptional circumstances – it could be beneficial for the provision to exist. Needless to say, the Association does not ever condone leaks to the media and I believe that the overall reputation of civil servants is secure in this regard.

Compellability of Witnesses

We are also concerned with the provisions of the Oireachtas (Compellability, Privileges and Immunities of Witnesses) Act. The Act distinguishes, in our view wrongfully, between the evidence that civil servants may give to an Oireachtas committee and that of other witnesses.

In section 1 of the Act 'evidence' is defined as including the expression of an opinion, belief, intention or allegation. Nevertheless, in Section 14 civil servants are not permitted to give evidence in this full sense. They are legally precluded from questioning or expressing an opinion on the merits of any policy of the government or a minister of the government or the Attorney General or on the objectives of such policy. This restriction would not apply in respect of evidence in the Courts or before a tribunal of inquiry and, in a situation where individual civil servants may now be designated by law to be responsible for particular areas, this could be a problem. Given the significance of the appearance before an Oireachtas committee to personal and professional character and reputation, the limitations in the Act are a diminution of civil rights.

The characters and reputations of civil servants are as precious as anyone else's and their rights must be respected. This is all-important in a legal environment in which individual named civil servants will be publicly accountable for assigned functions.

Strategic Management

The intention is that strategy statements and business plans in departments would be linked through a performance management system to individual objectives and performances in departments. Henry Mintzberg in his book, *The Rise and Fall of Strategic Planning*, begins one of the chapters with the following quotation:

I was in a warm bed, and suddenly I am part of a plan
Woody Allen in *Shadow and Fog*

There may well be individuals in the public service who feel somewhat like Woody Allen, but strategic management is here to stay and we fundamentally support it. Having said that, the reality is that the strategy statements published before the enactment of the Public Service Management Act were not exactly best sellers and would I believe in some cases be perceived to be somewhat inward-looking and aspirational.

A central key to success is the new performance management process and its link to individual and team goals within Business Plans and Strategy Statements. It is imperative that the focus is on continuous involvement in getting the job done, performing and managing better, and not on filling in annual rating boxes. It is imperative that the process is supported through serious investment in training and development.

It is most important that the strategic management process does not get bogged down in committees, in paper and in consultants. The tendency, particularly in bureaucratic organisations, is to focus on the process rather than on what needs to be changed to meet the requirements of the external environment and the public. Unless the SMI delivers a better quality of service it will have failed. Unless it becomes part of the culture and not just an add-on it will have failed.

There is still a real need to keep it simple and to communicate better in departments. To take a simple quality of service example, it would be better for everyone to sign up to answering telephones within, say, not more than five rings rather than have a glossy Customer Charter which is unachievable because the government might not put the money in to providing friendly accommodation to relieve queues!

Turning to consultants; I do not want to sound too cynical, but in my thirty years of experience in the public service I have rarely seen a solution put forward by consultants which did not, in some respects, make the simplest proposition esoteric and did not require the continued involvement of consultants for future success. The ownership of change and the control of that change must be firmly placed in the hands of the various stakeholders in the civil service. The success of the change effort should be measured by the extent to which it becomes internally self-sufficient.

Assignment of Responsibilities and Functions

The Public Service Management Act provides for the assignment of the responsibilities for the performance of functions to officers or to a grade or grades of officers of a department. The officer or grade to whom the assignment is made will be accountable to the secretary general.

The assignments are very broadly based, encompassing all aspects of responsibility for the work area concerned. A difficulty that arises is the extent to which the level of performance required under the Act may be aspirational, against a background of severely limited resources and the inability on the part of officers to control resources.

Civil servants will want to be satisfied under this new legal model of accountability that they are not going to end up being responsible when things go wrong and the ministers or, for that matter secretaries general, responsible when things go right. There is a growing culture of blame and, certainly, so far as my association is concerned, we will have to be satisfied that our members are not put in an impossible situation by virtue of unrealistic legal assignments.

The Partnership Approach

This leads me naturally to the issue of partnership and the consensus approach that has existed between the government and the unions over the past ten years. It should go without saying that any failure by the government to live up to its commitments in relation to promised taxation or other reforms would end the consensus. Equally any further attempt to ignore or undermine restructuring agreements in the civil service would be fatal. Industrial peace is an essential prerequisite to managing change, and my association's view is that the front door rather than the back door use of arbitration on pay issues is the best guarantee of industrial peace in the public service.

The current agreement, *Partnership 2000*, provides for partnership models to be developed both at national and local levels and arrangements are being put in hand in this regard. Let me just say this. If the government want partnership on SMI, they have to be serious and actually use the partnership structures. The Public Service Management Act was published without even being shown to the Co-ordinating Group on Strategic Management. And, speaking personally as a member of that group, I wonder at the infrequency at which it meets and the extent to which, in practice, decisions are being taken outside of it.

If partnership is to work then the old departmental model under which management on high 'decided' and then 'consulted' down the line will have to change. Equally the tendency on the union side to see everything in pay terms (the AHCS as a union exclusively representing management grades is above this pecuniary interest!) will have to change. It is vital that co-ownership between management, unions and staff is developed. Consensus has to be seen to move from the national to the local level.

I referred earlier to the need for a board type structure in the management of departments. This structure should be replicated in a cascading manner down the line in departments. The new performance management system should incorporate regular meetings at divisional, sectional and team level so that there is a common understanding of what must be done and of the individual responsibilities and interdependencies.

Terms and Conditions of Employment

There are draft proposals for change under the Public Service Management Act in relation to the appointment and dismissal of civil servants. Our association represents both principals and assistant principals and we are opposed to the distinction in relation to treatment which is signalled in the Act. Assistant principals, as their name

117

implies, are regularly involved in the full range of principal duties including, where appropriate, dealing with ministers on policy, legislation and other items. They should not be treated differently.

Changes are proposed in the 1956 Civil Service Commission and Civil Service Regulation Acts. In the normal course of industrial relations, we are entitled to expect that any changes in the terms and conditions of employment of civil servants will first be discussed with the civil service trade unions, and that there will be no question of unilaterally imposed change. There are, of course, also very important legal rights that have to be respected. While there is always internal criticism, some of it fair and some of it not so fair, we might remember that the Irish civil service is held in the highest regard internationally – and not just in relation to political impartiality, honesty and integrity; there is also considerable respect for administrative efficiency and the commitment and dedication in carrying out the job in hands.

Conclusion

I have touched on issues of concern from a trade union perspective. There are others that will arise as time goes on. There is a common interest in progressing in a manner that respects legitimate views on both sides. The real challenge is how to ensure that the core values of the public service are carried forward under a new model. Public service is more than a job – it is a vocation. Those who advocate more radical change need to be careful that they do not undermine the sense of commitment and integrity – the philosophy that a life of service, to the best of one's ability, to community and country is a life well spent.